Is Canada Even Real?

Is Canada Even Real?

HOW A NATION BUILT ON HOBOS, BEAVERS, WEIRDOS, AND HIP HOP CONVINCED THE WORLD TO BELIEBE

J.C. VILLAMERE

DUNDURN
TORONTO

Cover image credits: front — Muriel McDonald; back — Peter Puck screengrabs, NBC/CBC
Printer: Marquis

Library and Archives Canada Cataloguing in Publication

Villamere, J. C., author
    Is Canada even real? : how a nation built on hobos, beavers, weirdos, and hip hop convinced the world to beliebe
/ J.C. Villamere.

Includes bibliographical references and index.
Issued in print and electronic formats.
ISBN 978-1-4597-3883-6 (softcover).--ISBN 978-1-4597-3884-3 (PDF).--ISBN 978-1-4597-3885-0 (EPUB)

  1. National characteristics, Canadian--Humor. 2. Canada--
History--Humor. I. Title.

FC97.V54 2017   971   C2016-907646-6
                                           C2016-907647-4

1   2   3   4   5   21   20   19   18   17

We acknowledge the support of the **Canada Council for the Arts** and the **Ontario Arts Council** for our publishing program. We also acknowledge the financial support of the **Government of Ontario**, through the **Ontario Book Publishing Tax Credit** and the **Ontario Media Development Corporation**, and the **Government of Canada**.

Care has been taken to trace the ownership of copyright material used in this book. The author and the publisher welcome any information enabling them to rectify any references or credits in subsequent editions.

— *J. Kirk Howard, President*

The publisher is not responsible for websites or their content unless they are owned by the publisher.

Printed and bound in Canada.

VISIT US AT

dundurn.com | @dundurnpress | dundurnpress | dundurnpress

Dundurn
3 Church Street, Suite 500
Toronto, Ontario, Canada
M5E 1M2

For Peter and Bea

Contents

Introduction

Is Canada even real?

It's a question that is being asked with increasing frequency as those outside our borders become aware of our water-proof, see-through, mythically maple-scented currency and our improbably hot prime minister's assertions that Santa lives here.

In an age of wiki, Google Maps, and #factcheck, how could the very existence of Canada be questioned? And yet, how could a nation built on beaver pelts exist in the same realm as, say, Belgium or Niger?

In May 2015, the *National Post* (one of three national papers located *in* Canada) ran an article entitled "Experts Agree: Canada Is a Real Country." On the other hand, an ongoing argument at Debate.org addresses the question, "If you die in Canada, do you die in real life?" Currently, 79 percent of respondents say no.

At first glance, the cultural touchpoints covered in this book — hobos, beavers, hip hop, weirdos, and mascots — may seem scattershot. But upon closer consideration, these are no less random than a book that examines maple leaves, hockey, canoes, totem poles, and polar bears. This second collection of topics likely hangs more closely together in your mind as a reflection of Canada. But why? Consider this: if Canada's true cultural physiognomies made perfect sense to the common observer, few would debate its existence.

This book invites you to look past our past and see that Canada is no longer solely the icons in which we once saw ourselves. Fragments of Canada can be represented by lighthouses, totem poles, and inukshuks, but Canada is at its realest in the minutia of our shared memories and culture.

This book offers a petri dish of our culture for your inspection and reflection. It examines the factors behind the twenty-first-century monolithic myth of Canada, a nation that is wise, silly, and real — even if only in your imagination.

Is Canada even real? Let's find out.

— J.C. Villamere (rhymes with "spill-a-beer")

ROUND ONE
Hobos

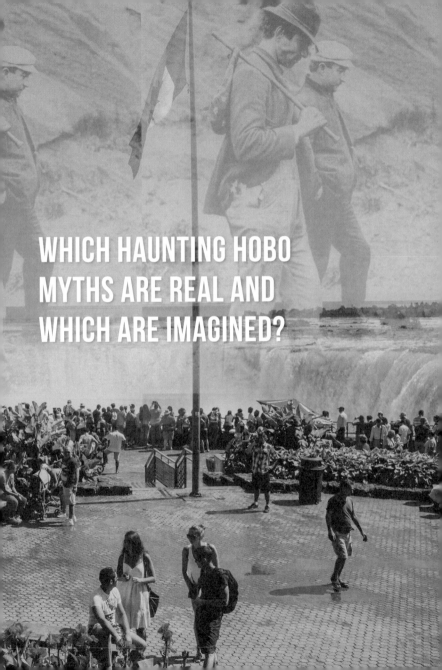

WHICH HAUNTING HOBO MYTHS ARE REAL AND WHICH ARE IMAGINED?

THE LITTLEST HOBO:
OUR GERMAN SHEPHERD
GUARDIAN ANGEL TV STAR

The year is 1979. Margaret Thatcher dramatically wins the British general election, becoming the first female prime minister of Britain. Skylab, NASA's first orbiting space station, returns triumphantly to Earth after soaring through the stars for more than six miraculous years. Pope John Paul II's trip to his homeland of Poland sparks a revolution of conscience that transforms a nation.

Meanwhile, in Canada, television executives in Toronto launch a program that stars a

German shepherd that travels from town to town befriending clowns, rescuing ballerinas, and foiling gold robbers.

On Thursday, October 11, 1979, *The Littlest Hobo* (French title: *Le Vagabond*) premieres on CTV. The pilot episode begins, as each episode will, with Terry Bush's urban hymn "Maybe Tomorrow." While most other dramas and comedies are shot on film, *The Littlest Hobo* is recorded on hard, cheap, bright videotape, a medium reserved for ephemeral (read: disposable) programming.

The opening credits are comprised of a modular montage that shows us, variously, Hobo trotting down a suburban street, Hobo running out of the woods, Hobo in the passenger seat of a convertible. He does not look glamorous, even in a convertible. He is all business. But he is not a business dog. We know this because he wears no tie, no glasses, has no briefcase. "Just grab a hat, we'll travel light, that's hobo style," sings Bush, a wistful smile in his voice. But Hobo wears no hat. Not even a collar. Potentially the least anthropomorphized animal to ever capture the imaginations of both young and old, this dog never wears clothes and is known only as "Hobo," or by nicknames bestowed by his short-term human companions.

The show's title appears in yellow brush-stroke font: The LITTLEST HOBO. Say "the"; YELL THE REST.

We see Hobo leading a cow, Hobo placing a call, Hobo carrying a rifle. He swims in a lake, his ears smoothed against his nape. He is always moving, always onward. Hobo runs out of the woods, tongue out, panting as he surveys the scene. The next title card reads: Starring LONDON. (Yell it!)

A rainbow-bright hot-air balloon sits in the air. Is Hobo aboard? Wait, Hobo is swimming across a stream now; he emerges onto a rocky outcrop and shakes the water from his coat. Droplets of water arc out in all directions. It is a dramatic visual. It is the most dramatic visual you will see for the duration of the program. A dog shaking water off himself. Hold on to that. Hold dearly to that sense of wonder, that action.

Hobo's origins, motivation, and ultimate destination are never explained over the course of the series. In this capacity, he is the perfect metaphor for Canada.

In the opening scene of the pilot episode of *The Littlest Hobo*, our altruistic Alsatian befriends forest ranger Ray Caldwell and rescues a pair of wildcat cubs from a forest fire. But the scene is soft, slow, halting. There are no subtle nuances. There are broad actions and sharp transitions. There is no budget for suspense.

As the episode continues, a local storekeeper aims to keep the forest's fire-ravaged animals at bay by setting a trap of raw hamburger laced with rat poison outside his shop, but it's eaten by a toddler. First of all, I hope viewers made note that CTV was the destination on Thursday evenings for watching wee ones eat raw meat, but secondly, and most importantly, *Where were you on that one, Hobo?*

In an attempt to save the child, Ranger Caldwell and Hobo set off by plane to fetch a doctor and the antidote, but a thunderstorm prevents Caldwell from landing the plane back home, leading to this tense exchange:

Caldwell: Of all the rough luck. I can't even see the airstrip.

The doctor: What can we do?

Caldwell: The only other place is about ten miles out. We might make it there, but there wouldn't be any kind of vehicle to go the rest of the way.

The doctor: The child needs an antidote in a hurry.

Caldwell: Doc, can you fly a plane?

The doctor: Goodness, no, no, I've only been up a few times in my life. Why?

Caldwell: There's a parachute in the rear. You could land it and I could jump with the antidote.

The doctor: Sorry.[1]

You're likely now considering that scriptwriting might be a much, much easier venture than you'd previously imagined, and it may prove to be a generous source of income for you or anyone else capable of penning such prose — say, your nine-year-old tabby or your great aunt with the acquired brain injury. With characteristic Canadian humility, even those behind the scenes acknowledged that aspects of the show were lacking. "Sometimes the stories, quite honestly, may fall flat," producer Barrie Diehl

---

1 "Smoke," *The Littlest Hobo*, CTV Television, 1979.

told *StarWeek* in 1985. "It could be considered unexciting.… *The A-Team* is exciting. They shoot guns."

Returning to the show, we see that, naturally, Caldwell and the doctor take the only reasonable course of action under the circumstances: they strap a parachute to the stray and hurl it out of the plane in a storm.

"You know, I could swear you've done this before," Caldwell says to the dog with a cure for poisoning attached to his collar and a parachute strapped to his back. Our four-legged hero hops out of the plane as the ranger whispers, "Good luck."

The chute deploys and Hobo comes to a reasonably graceless landing in a field. He sprints through a forest and across a creek.

We see the toddler's anxious parents waiting in a medical clinic. Then Hobo walks into the clinic and the attendant immediately goes for his neck pack. Obviously, this dog is here with the cure. A perfunctory "good dog" is issued. The toddler is saved. Now, Hobo rests.

Only one question remains: How is this even a real show? Oh, and also, all these other questions:

• • • • • • • • • • • • • • •

1. Which of these Canadian celebrities guest-starred on *The Littlest Hobo*?
   a) Super Dave Osborne
   b) Mike Myers
   c) David Suzuki
   d) Leslie Nielsen

• • • • • • • • • • • • • • •

2. How many episodes of *The Littlest Hobo* were produced by CTV?
   a) 18
   b) 50
   c) 67
   d) 114

3. **What happens in the final episode of the series?**

   a) Hobo finds an undetonated Second World War bomb

   b) a gambler plans to sabotage a lumberjack contest

   c) a criminal tries to sell a stolen secret laser

   d) Hobo is mistaken for a sheep-killing wolf

4. **Reruns of *The Littlest Hobo* ran on national networks until**

   a) the '80s

   b) the '90s

   c) the '00s

   d) the '10s

5. **The program is based on**

   a) a 1958 Hollywood movie about a stray dog that befriends a boy named Tommy and rescues his pet lamb from slaughter

   b) *Le Vagabond*, a Quebecois fairy tale that also features a man who believes himself to be a horse

   c) an acid-fuelled fever dream endured by television producer Dorrell McGowan

   d) the 1978 TV series *Incredible Hulk*, which sees a widowed traveller help others in need despite his terrible secret

6. **London, the dog who played Hobo, co-starred with Prince in which film?**

   a) *Purple Rain*

   b) *Under the Cherry Moon*

   c) *Graffiti Bridge*

   d) *The Sacrifice of Victor*

ANSWERS

• • • • • • • • • • • • • •
1. **Which of these Canadian celebrities guest-starred on** *The Littlest Hobo*?

Answer: d) Leslie Nielsen

You get a full mark for Leslie Nielsen, the Regina-born actor who gained cred as a dramatic actor in movies like *Forbidden Planet* and *The Poseidon Adventure* before coming into his own as one of film's finest deadpan comedians in sublimely absurd films like *Airplane!* and the *Naked Gun* franchise.

Nielsen played it straight as Mayor Chester Montgomery in season 1, episode 19, "Romiet and Julio," which originally aired March 20, 1980, and tells the story of Hobo saving the fate of star-crossed love.

Regina's Leslie Nielsen of *Littlest Hobo* fame chills on an *Airplane!*

Award yourself half a point if you answered Mike Myers. The Scarborough super-hoser never officially guest-starred on *The Littlest Hobo,* but he did have a cameo in season 1, episode 10, "Boy on Wheels," in which Hobo helps a paraplegic boy enter a

Frisbee contest, much to the chagrin of the boy's dad, who has hated dogs ever since he swerved his car to avoid a stray and instead crashed, killing his wife and maiming his son (another typical Hobo plot of light fare the whole family can enjoy). Myers plays the boy's buddy, Tommy. The credited guest star for this episode is Clarence Williams III, best known as the *Mod Squad* cop with the sweet Afro.

Although Bob Einstein's luckless stuntman character Super Dave got his start on CTV's early '80s sketch comedy show *Bizarre* and parlayed his popularity into the Global TV series *The Super Dave Osborne Show* (1987–92), Einstein isn't even Canadian — he was born in Los Angeles. This interloper has never appeared on *The Littlest Hobo*.

David Suzuki is a Canadian academic, science broadcaster, environmental activist, and national treasure. Since 1979, he's hosted the CBC science program *The Nature of Things*, which is seen in more than forty countries. Surely he's too urbane to appear in the unsophisticated canine caper that is *The Littlest Hobo*. Instead, he guest-starred on *The Beachcombers* in the 1981 episode "The Tray Tree," playing himself.

• • • • • • • • • • • • • •

2. How many episodes of *The Littlest Hobo* were produced by CTV?

Answer: d) 114

CTV shot a whopping 114 episodes, with plots that ranged from Hobo befriending a vaudevillian kleptomaniac to Hobo finding a truckload(!) of diamonds to Hobo helping a farmer and his mute daughter break free of a blackmail scheme that forces them to conduct fake séances. Classic.

• • • • • • • • • • • • • • •

3. What happens in the final episode of the series?

Answer: a) Hobo finds an undetonated Second World War bomb

Hobo finds the undetonated bomb in the final episode, "Pandora," which aired March 7, 1985. I won't reveal how the episode is resolved, but it was Hobo's last adventure. David Glyn-Jones guest-starred. "The theatre is a savage mistress," he said. "She dangles great joys before you, then frequently snatches them away before you can satisfy yourself." Revelatory words from a man who also guest-starred on *The Beachcombers*. Twice.

• • • • • • • • • • • • • • •

4. Reruns of *The Littlest Hobo* ran on national networks until

Answer: d) the '10s

The series aired on CTV on Thursday nights at 7:30 p.m. from 1979 to 1985. Reruns continued on CTV, CTV Two, and other national networks up until the early 2010s. Many episodes can now be viewed in their entirety on YouTube.

• • • • • • • • • • • • • • •

5. The program is based on

Answer: a) a 1958 Hollywood movie about a stray dog that befriends a boy named Tommy and rescues his pet lamb from slaughter

The Littlest Hobo is based on the 1958 movie of the same name. The film stars a sixteen-year-old

The Littlest Hobo hangs on set with his lamb co-star.

did not choose to return to his roots with a guest appearance on *The Littlest Hobo*; instead, he branched out and worked on stunts in over a hundred movies, including *The Outsiders, Scarface, The 40-Year-Old Virgin, Grindhouse,* and *Django Unchained*. In retrospect, he sounds like the kind of guy who should have been able to protect his own pet lamb.

The Littlest Hobo was first adapted for the small screen in the 1960s. The initial series was shot in West Vancouver and other locales around British Columbia and aired from 1963 to 1965 in black and white on CTV. It was billed as a slick action show and marketed to adults. The show's 1979 revival was sometimes referred to as *The New Littlest Hobo*.

Chuck Eisenmann was the talented, gentle dog trainer

Buddy Joe Hooker as Tommy. Hooker went on to become a Hollywood actor who guest-starred on shows including *Leave It to Beaver, Charlie's Angels, Magnum, P.I., Columbo,* and *Baywatch*. In his '80s heyday he who owned the stars of all three incarnations. The top star was London, but his relatives Toro, Litlon, and Thorn also played scenes as the Hobo. On his philosophy of dog training, Eisenmann said, "A dog thinks just as a human does, and if you treat him as a stupid animal eventually he will act that way. That's why I act positive around my dogs and treat them as friends." Sounds very friendly and Canadian, doesn't it? Eisenmann was born in Roseburg, Oregon, but his baseball career landed him stints with the Vancouver Capilanos

and the Ottawa Giants in the early '50s, so let's claim some of his warm personality as our own doing, shall we?

. . . .

6. London, the dog who plays Hobo, co-starred with Prince in which film?

Answer: c) *Graffiti Bridge*

I know. You're disappointed it wasn't *Purple Rain*. Take heart though: *Graffiti Bridge*, Prince's 1990 critical and commercial musical disaster, was the sequel to *Purple Rain*.

2

SOL: THE HOBO CLOWN OF *PARLEZ-MOI/* YOUR NIGHTMARES

The FLQ, asbestos, Oka, separatism, the Expos: Quebec has had its share of horrifying crises. But nothing has done so much so fast to imprint the horrors of *la belle province* on a generation of Canadians as Sol, an unintentionally terrifying hobo clown character created by Quebecois comedic actor Marc Favreau.

Favreau and his alter ego Sol starred in *Parlez-Moi* ("Talk to Me"), a French instructional show for anglophone children that debuted on TVOntario in 1978. That same year, Pogo the

Killer Clown's alter ego, John Wayne Gacy, was charged with murdering thirty-three young people, and *Halloween* was released, the hit slasher film that showed a clown-costumed six year old killing his sis with a kitchen knife. It was a banner year for coulrophobia.

In each episode of *Parlez-Moi*, Favreau appears as himself, speaking English with a thick Quebec accent to introduce viewers to new French words and phrases. For example, in the episode "Sol in the Restaurant," he offers instruction on how to order a seven-course meal. Favreau shares the French translations for such preschool mealtime favourites as "meat paste," soup, beef, salad, a cheese course, and fruit. One surefire way to put someone off pâté is to introduce it as meat paste. To turn toddlers off of the idea of French food forever, show them that fruit constitutes dessert.

Other episodes in the series demonstrate even less attention to how French might be used in preschoolers' everyday lives. In the episode "Sol Goes Through Customs," children learn such handy phrases as "I have nothing to declare," and "I don't smoke." It's logical to conclude that the target market was lost in translation during the program's development.

After Favreau's brief French lesson, he introduces an entirely French sketch in which Sol the Clown uses the new vocabulary in situ. Sol wears the diamond-patterned shirt of a playing-card jester and a clashing necktie beneath a frayed, heavily patched trench coat. His hat can best be described as garbage. He wears a beard of brown make-up, and his drawn-on

eyebrows circle down around his eyes to become deep bags beneath. He shows more chest hair than a present-day children's entertainer would be encouraged to.

In "Sol in the Restaurant," the waiter does not hesitate to seat this ridiculous caricature of a homeless person in his swanky French bistro. The waiter asks how many are in Sol's party. He answers, *Je suis seul* (I am alone), but he bends the pronunciation just enough for it to be heard as, *Je suis Sol* (I am Sol). This clever wordplay is lost on the show's target audience, who instead learn one more reason to fear clowns and make an unconscious mental note to drop French.

Like *The Littlest Hobo*, *Parlez-Moi* is shot on video, but with production values that make

Esstradinaire! indeed: Sol is celebrated in his home province.

Hobo's look refined. The colour saturation is cranked up to hallucinatory levels. The audio is recorded so closely you can hear Favreau smile.

In addition to the terms and phrases that Favreau has introduced, Sol's sketches feature a ton of other French words used quickly against a visual backdrop of corny gags and slapstick stylings that highlight the chasm between English and French comedic sensibilities.

The waiter shows Sol to his table and says, *asseyez-vous* (sit down). Sol sits *on* the table, knocking it over and spilling its settings dramatically on the floor. For added comic effect, Sol tries to take a bite out of the tablecloth.

- FIN -

To a generation of anglophone Canadians, Sol is a personality they forgot they remembered, along with how to conjugate the verb *avoir* and the difference between *sus* and *sous*. But to generations of francophone Canadians, Sol is a hero, and the late Marc Favreau is considered a genius.

Favreau has been beloved in Quebec since he first introduced the character of Sol on the long-running Radio Canada children's program *La Boîte à Surprise* (the Surprise Box) in 1958. In a French program aimed at a French audience, the character connected immediately.

Today, it would be considered inappropriate for a children's entertainer to create a clown character based on an impoverished migratory worker, but hobos made relatively frequent appearances in the cartoons of the '40s and '50s in such popular series as *Looney Tunes* and *Merrie Melodies*. It was in this era that Favreau created Sol.

By 1974, Favreau had developed Sol's monologues into a sophisticated, philosophical, and

Bibliothèque Marc-Favreau in Montreal.

enormously popular one-man show geared toward French adults. The hobo clown poetically reflected on politics, the environment, education, love, and death with elaborate and ingenious yet wholly untranslatable French turns of phrase and *jeux de mots.* He toured Quebec and France to great acclaim.

A classically trained actor, Favreau had a penchant for absurdist drama, a genre in which tension is often found when characters lack the communication skills to understand their surroundings. Many absurdist plays, such as Harold Pinter's *The Room* and *The Birthday Party,* show characters trapped in an enclosed space and contending with a force they can't understand. Through this lens, viewers can see that in every episode of *Parlez-Moi*, Sol is the menacing yet pathos-filled force.

Favreau was made a knight of the National Order of Quebec in 1995 and an officer of the Order of Canada in 2003. He received the Prix de la Francophonie from the Société des Auteurs Dramatiques de Paris in 2000. In his hometown of Montreal, a new library bears his name and incorporates artwork inspired by Sol. Favreau's career is considered a masterpiece.

In this light, Sol becomes a concept for illustrating the long-held notion of Canada as a country of two solitudes: French and English Canada are separated by a lack of understanding and mutual indifference. There is wordplay to be found here, a linguistic barrel race that would cross the finish line with a perfect congregation and corrugation, neatly pleating the name of Sol into the phrase "two solitudes" — if only Favreau, who passed in 2005, was here to conjure it.

Instead, we turn to these quiz questions:

• • • • • • • • • • • • • • •

1. **True or False: Cirque du Soleil mounted a production inspired by and named after Sol.**

• • • • • • • • • • • • • • •

2. **How many seasons of *Parlez-Moi* did TVOntario produce?**
   a) 1
   b) 2
   c) 5
   d) 10

• • • • • • • • • • • • • • •

3. **True or False: *Parlez-Moi* also aired in the United States.**

• • • • • • • • • • • • • • • • •

4. **The character of Sol is inspired by:**
   a) a character in *Waiting for Godot*
   b) the celebrated Swiss clown Grock
   c) the French clown Cha-U-Kao, who was a performer at the Moulin Rouge
   d) the American TV clown Rusty Nails

• • • • • • • • • • • • • • • •

5. **True or false: Marc Favreau was a self-taught painter who made more money from his lithographs of clowns than he did from his career as a performer.**

Answers

• • • • • • • • • • • • • • •

1. True or False: Cirque du
   Soleil mounted a production
   inspired by and named after
   Sol.

Answer: False

Despite 2011 reports from the
satirical news site *The O-Dot*,
the Montreal-based circus theatre company did not create a
Sol production in the vein of
their Michael Jackson-, Elvis-,
and Beatles-inspired projects.
Although a clown character
like Sol might seem like a natural fit for the type of modern,
character-based circus show that
Cirque excels at, Sol's charms stem
from his playful way with words,
and Cirque's productions generally rely on music in place of dialogue. Also, as Ontarian children

of the '80s can attest, no matter
what ingenious verbal manoeuvres
Sol employs, he cannot clear the
hurdle of the French-English language barrier.

• • • • • • • • • • • • • • •

2. How many seasons of *Parlez-
   Moi* did TVOntario produce?

Answer: b) 2

TVOntario produced two seasons
of *Parlez-Moi* from 1978 to 1980.
Season 1 was comprised of sixty
ten-minute episodes that covered
topics ranging from the genuinely
worrisome "Sol and the Scout
Tent" to the implausible "Sol
Buys a House" to the inevitable
"Sol Goes to Court." Episodes in
season 2 were expanded from ten
minutes to fifteen and included
more hobo-appropriate adventures, including "Sol on the Bus,"
"Sol at the Train Station," and
"Sol in the Park."

• • • • • • • • • • • • • • •

3. True or False: *Parlez-Moi* also aired in the United States.

Answer: True

Louisiana Public Broadcasting aired the program in the 1980s as a way to help preserve the region's francophone heritage and to support the French-immersion education of students there. In 2016, the broadcaster announced a content partnership with Télévision Française de l'Ontario (TFO), the French-language educational television network that grew out of TVOntario, presumably to continue the international partnership spurred by *Parlez-Moi* and its commitment to its legacy of providing impenetrably French programming to unsettled children. *C'est formidable!*

• • • • • • • • • • • • • • •

4. The character of Sol is inspired by

Answer: a) a poet tramp in *Waiting for Godot*

According to Claude Fournier, who created *La Boîte à Surprise*, the show that launched Sol, the character was inspired by Estragon, who together with Vladimir awaited Godot in Samuel Beckett's classic play. In Act 1, Vladimir tells Estragon he should have been a poet. Estragon gestures to his ragged clothes and replies, "I was."

• • • • • • • • • • • • • • •

5. True or false: Marc Favreau was a self-taught painter who made more money from his lithographs of clowns than he did from his career as a performer.

Answer: False

That's the story of another hobo clown. Red Skelton, the American radio and television star of the '40s, '50s, and '60s, introduced his hobo clown character Freddie the Freeloader in 1952. Skelton painted clowns as a hobby until 1964, when he launched his first art exhibition in Las Vegas. The show was a success and sales of his original oil paintings, prints, and lithographs reportedly earned the performer, who died in 1997, about $2.5 million annually.

3

WILF CARTER:
MARITIME COWBOY
AND HOBO BALLADEER

Semantics matter. A hobo is not to be confused with a bum or a tramp. Yes, all three are homeless and jobless, but how they apply these conditions to their lifestyle matters. Hobos — or as their less train-bound, more modern equivalents are referred to, migrant workers or migratory labourers — travel from town to town trying to pick up work. A tramp travels but doesn't work, and a bum just loafs around. Some etymological sources claim that "bum" derives from the German verb *bummeln*, which

The Venn diagram of work-loaf balance

in search of work. By the 1960s the phenomenon had all but disappeared, thanks to the rise of social welfare and the economic upswing bolstered by the Second World War. A *Globe and Mail* reporter in 1964 lamented that he

means to loaf around or saunter, but popular agreement determines it more likely reflects the synonym for "arse." At any rate, there is a hierarchy at play here, with hobos at the top.

The railway-riding hobo lifestyle emerged in the 1860s following the end of the American Civil War and reached its peak during the Great Depression in the 1930s as people took to riding the rails across the country

A pair of genuine, 14-carat hobos.

hadn't encountered "a genuine, 14-carat hobo" for years.

It was during the era of the 14-carat hobo that country music emerged as a popular genre, and Wilf Carter rode this cultural zeitgeist to stardom as a country star who sang hobo songs.

Born in the fishing village of Port Hilford, Nova Scotia, in 1904, Carter caught the show-biz bug as a youth after seeing a yodeller perform. No, seriously: the foundation of country music is built out of the dreams of hobos, cowboys, and yodellers.

What is a yodel? Technically, it's a vocal technique in which you quickly and repeatedly alternate between a baritone range and a falsetto. Imagine wavering back and forth between the bass voice of Brad Roberts of the Crash Test Dummies and the crystal-clear high notes of the Weeknd. Okay, now put on a cowboy hat and eat beans from a can. You're getting there.

The rural European tradition of yodelling made its unlikely foray into the realm of entertainment long before those Ricola cough-drop TV ads bewitched you.

It was popular in vaudeville and music halls through the late 1800s and into the 1900s. The undulating vocal technique

Alphorns like the Ricola-style one pictured proved difficult for hobos to fit in their bindles.

can be heard in Patsy Cline's recordings in the '50s and '60s and in the work of successors like k.d. lang and LeAnn Rimes, whose 1996 hit "Blue" is positively yodel-rific. All owe a debt to American country music pioneer Jimmie Rodgers, who in 1928 released "Blue Yodel No. 1," which vaulted yodelling to craze-level popularity and launched Rodgers as country music's first-ever star.

RIDING ● MOUNTAINEERING ● FISHING
HOLIDAYS IN **CANADA**

A 1925 advertisement for Canadian Pacific.

By his mid-teens, Carter had peaced-out of Nova Scotia to live as a lumberjack hobo, honing his musical talents and teaching himself guitar in the aurally pleasing acoustic environment of a boxcar. By age twenty, he was an Alberta-based cowboy who moonlighted as a singing guitar player who performed at dances and other events.

He made his radio debut in 1930 on Calgary's fledgling CKMX, and by 1932 he'd secured a seemingly tailor-made gig from Canadian Pacific Railway to play and sing for tourists during horseback outings in the Canadian Rockies.

He managed to parlay this into an engagement as an entertainer

Our hobo hero Wilf Carter serenades tourists in the Rockies.

on the maiden voyage of the Canadian Pacific's SS *Empress of Britain*, the era's largest, fastest, and most luxurious transatlantic passenger ship between England and Canada.

During a stop in Montreal, he hopped off to record the yodel-laden country songs "My Swiss Moonlight Lullaby" and "The Capture of Albert Johnson." On the strength of the record, he

CANADIAN PACIFIC

EMPRESS STEAMERS
FAST LUXURIOUS
SERVICE TO CANADA

SEABORNE & BRYER, Shipping Agents, 9 South Street,
DORCHESTER, Dorset.

A 1920 ad for the *Empress*.

signed with RCA Victor and the album became a bestseller within a year.

Carter's sentimental ballads of farming, family, cowboy traditions, and the hobo life were delivered in a smooth, reedy voice over a rhythmic bass strum pattern on acoustic guitar. His gentle, simple three-chord wonders could be considered corny in retrospect, but there remains a quaint authenticity and a timeless quality to a song about the majestic pleasure of a bird at the window. (Audiences of the time agreed: Carter had a hit in 1949 with "There's a Bluebird on Your Windowsill.")

Among the many hobo songs Carter recorded are "I Ain't Gonna Be a Hobo No More," "The Hobo's Song to the Mounties," "The Hobo's Blues," "The Hobo's Dream of Heaven," and "The Hobo's Yodel."

Carter was the first Canadian country performer to top the charts. Then it was time for him to blaze another trail — the long-since-beaten track Canadian entertainers take south to the States to pursue fame and fortune on a scale that is, if not grander, at least larger.

As George Bernard Shaw observed, Canada and the United States are two countries divided by a shared language. Here it's a housecoat; there it's called a bathrobe. Here it's a serviette; there it's called a napkin. Here he is Wilf Carter; there they call him Montana Slim.

To modern ears, the name Wilf conjures an image of an old man, which makes sense: the name Wilfred was a common choice for baby boys in 1904. It's easily shortened to Will or Fred or Wilf, but seemingly none of these held the cachet of *Montana*, a name that was suggested to Carter by a CBS Radio lawyer.

The "nicknamification" of country stars was nothing new. Former railway workman Jimmie Rogers had been dubbed "The Singing Brakeman." Carter's protégé and fellow Nova Scotia–born yodelling country star Hank Snow was called "The Yodelling Ranger."

Carter had at times been called "The Singing Cowboy" until that moniker was usurped by Gene Autry after he starred in the 1936 western *The Singing Cowboy*. A more relevant nickname for Autry would be "That Guy Who Made a Hit out of 'Rudolph the Red-Nosed Reindeer,'" but that didn't happen until 1950, and by that time dibs on nicknames had already been called.

Carter's stage name, "Montana Slim," is unusual in that it is used almost exclusively south of the border, as though the American public's taste could not have been swayed by a man with a name as humdrum as Wilf Carter, and only an evocative country-and-western moniker with a dash of outlandish Hollywood swagger could hold their attention.

To talk about Wilf Carter south of the border is to make a mental translation beforehand, as you would to order a rye and Coke (make that a Canadian whisky and Coke when ordering stateside), or to ask where you can throw your garbage ("Where can I spit out this American cheese?").

It was as Montana Slim that Wilf Carter became a star with his U.S. radio show, which, at the height of its popularity was syndicated to more than 250 stations across North America. By comparison, today's most ubiquitous radio program, *On Air with Ryan Seacrest*, is syndicated to just 130 stations across the U.S. and Canada. By the late 1930s, Carter was receiving ten thousand weekly fan letters. Just in time for Christmas of 1935, the Eaton's catalogue offered the "Wilf Carter guitar," a birch model that was made in Canada and bore Carter's signature.

After being sidelined for most of the '40s due to a back injury sustained in a serious car crash, Carter made a triumphant return to live performance at the 1950 CNE in Toronto. He received a hero's welcome at the Calgary Stampede in 1964 and was a regular performer on *The Tommy Hunter Show*.

Carter's legendary status was confirmed with his induction into the Nashville Songwriters Hall of Fame in 1971, the Canadian Country Music Hall of Fame in 1984, and the Canadian Music Hall of Fame in 1985. Of the many accolades he received, the one that would resonate most with Canadians is the Stompin' Tom Connors song, "Tribute to Wilf Carter."

But most modern Canadians have never heard of Wilf Carter,

or even of Montana Slim. Like the hobo lifestyle he immortalized, changing times have obscured his impact, and his legacy fades in the wind like a train whistle.

All that remain are his records, his legacy, and this quiz, which can help you pass the time as you're cowpoking or riding the rails. Take an extra point if you yodel your answers:

· · · · · · · · · · · · · · · ·

1. Who is credited with the quote, "A nation that forgets its past has no future"?
   a) Winston Churchill
   b) Kim Mitchell
   c) Elvis Stojko
   d) Dr. Lotta Hitschmanova

· · · · · · · · · · · · · · · ·

2. Wilf Carter developed his own yodelling style called
   a) echo yodel
   b) three-in-one
   c) bluegrass yodel
   d) both a) and b)

· · · · · · · · · · · · · · · ·

3. Tommy Hunter's nickname is
   a) Canada's Country Gentleman
   b) Canada's Gentle Countryman
   c) Canada's Central Chantryman
   d) Canada's Ryan Seacrest

· · · · · · · · · · · · · · · ·

4. A "hobo" in modern parlance most likely refers to
   a) a popular brand of shoes
   b) a style of women's handbag
   c) the Home Owners Bargain Outlet
   d) Via Rail train conductor groupies

Answers

. . . .

1. **Who is credited with the quote, "A nation that forgets its past has no future"?**

Answer: a) Winston Churchill

Leaders will forever speak to the importance of remembering war heroes. Canadian history teachers will annually tell the tale of Jacques Cartier. But folk heroes like Stompin' Tom Connors are charged with the task of remembering their own and beseeching the public to hear and remember.

. . . .

2. **Wilf Carter developed his own yodelling style called**

Answer: d) both a) and b)

Carter developed a unique style of yodelling, known both as the echo yodel and the three-in-one yodel, which sounded less traditional Alpine style (think "The Lonely Goatherd" from *The Sound of Music*) and more lonesome cowboy (à la Dwight Yoakam).

. . . .

3. **Tommy Hunter's nickname is**

Answer: a) Canada's Country Gentleman

The Tommy Hunter Show, hosted by Canada's Country Gentleman himself, aired Friday nights on CBC TV as a lead-in to American fare like *M*A*S*H* and *All in the Family*. Wilf Carter was a regular guest, and stars like Garth Brooks, Shania Twain (then known as Eileen Twain), The Judds, and Alanis Morissette also received early exposure on the program.

The long-running show began as a CBC radio program in 1960 and replaced *Country Hoedown* on CBC TV in 1965, where it aired until 1992.

• • • • • • • • • • • • • • •

4. A "hobo" in modern parlance most likely refers to

Answer: b) a style of women's handbag

While the term "hobo bag" would more logically describe the kerchief-and-stick contraption employed by cartoon hobos and referred to as a "bindle," the modern hobo bag refers to a large, rounded tote usually made of leather and used to carry sippy cups, debit cards, and cellphones instead of corncob pipes, cans of beans, and harmonicas.

4

HOBO WITH A SHOTGUN: VIGILANTE HOBO CANUXPLOITATION A-GO-GO

There are very few routines Canadians follow when they settle in to watch a domestic film. This is because there are very few Canadians who ever settle in to watch a domestic film. Sure, plenty of movies are filmed in Canada, but they're usually made by American filmmakers who contemptuously disguise Canadian locations as American towns.

Watching a Canadian movie almost never involves a Tuesday night popcorn date at the cineplex, because that hallowed church of motion pictures is reserved for

American movies. Instead, it's usually a matter of cajoling oneself to pay attention to a DVD from the public library. The main motivation is earning the right to say you watched *Atanarjuat: The Fast Runner* or *Bon Cop, Bad Cop* and to offer insightful reviews like "I watched the whole thing," and "It actually wasn't that bad."

There is one custom that Canadians generally adhere to on the rare occasions when they watch anything that's not just filmed here but also set here, and it is this: Canadians will parse every single frame for flashes of Canada. Any familiar landscape or landmark is excitedly noted in practical disbelief.

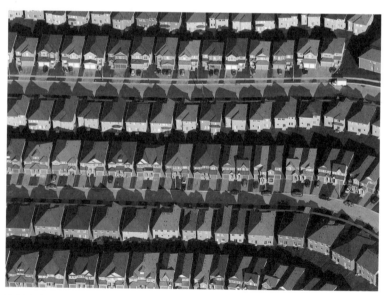

"I think I see my house!"

Such was the approach when viewing 2011's *Hobo with a Shotgun*. Filmed in Halifax and Dartmouth, Nova Scotia, and set in the fictional location of Hope Town, the film was branded as Canuxploitation, and its Canadian roots were not obscured but instead celebrated during the movie's marketing and release.

Canuxploitation! Finally, a hip term for a brave new breed of film that is unapologetically Canadian. Let's unpack this portmanteau of *Canuck* and *exploitation*:

1. *Canuck*: An affectionate name for our nationality that's also the official name of Vancouver's NHL team and the nickname for both our Avro CF-100 fighter jets and our men's rugby team. The term was also emblazoned on our official Vancouver 2010 Olympic gear, and who can forget the Crazy Canucks, our superstar '70s-era alpine ski racer team?

2. *Exploitation film*: A low-budget film that's built to exploit current trends, niche genres, or lurid content. Great! Canada has been waiting for over a century to take its rightful place in the annals of current trends.

At the outset, *Hobo with a Shotgun* seems even more flag-waving than 2010's *Scott Pilgrim vs. the World*, an American movie that functions as an unlikely valentine to its deliberate and prominent Toronto setting. Canadian viewers eagerly (SO EAGERLY) noted the appearance in that film of familiar places like Pizza Pizza, Casa Loma, Lee's Palace, and Second Cup, and rewound parts of the movie to ensure they could believe their eyes when legitimate Canadian currency was used onscreen. It is through this lens of optimistic national boosterism that *Hobo with a Shotgun* is viewed.

As the opening credits roll, we see the titular hobo character. The main character, called simply "He," is parka-clad and wearing a toque-and-stubble combo reminiscent of Relic from *The Beachcombers*. With the traditional hobo luggage of a bindle in hand, he rides a boxcar through bucolic Canadian scenery beautiful enough to challenge the footage that accompanies the national anthem in the sign-off Canadian TV channels used to play at the end of the broadcast day.

In the establishing scene, we see Robb Wells, best known as the lovable dope Ricky from the best-loved Canadian TV series, *Trailer Park Boys*. And is that Gregory Smith, better known as Dov Epstein from the reasonably watchable Global show *Rookie Blue*? It is! And so begins a joyous journey into a long-overdue, unabashed celebration of our nation on celluloid.

W-w-wait — why is Smith holding this bleak neighbourhood at gunpoint and forcing men, women, and children to watch while Wells is brutally and graphically yet gleefully decapitated by a barbed wire noose? *Anyone recognize that Halifax housing project?* A bikini-clad dancer in stilettos seductively writhes in the blood fountain erupting from his neck stump. *Is her swimsuit from Le Château's latest collection?* Wells's head is now a hood ornament. *Did anyone notice whether that car has Nova Scotia plates?* Hobo smashes a bottle over his own head. *Was that a Labatt's stubby?* An angry mob appears — look, they're carrying snow shovels and hockey

sticks instead of pitchforks. How Canadian! There's George Stroumboulopoulos … nope, he was just brutally murdered with a hockey skate thrown like a ninja star. Okay, Santa Claus is making an appearance. Santa is so Canadian. Prime Minister Trudeau insists he lives here. Oh. I see this Santa is a pedophile. And his crotch was just shot off. That's a tremendous amount of blood. There's blood all over everything.

Wait a second — this movie is not exploiting Canada at all! It's not *that* type of Canuxploitation. It's just a Canadian-made movie that gleefully exploits a dark carnival of gore and torture. It's less like affable CBC comedian Rick Mercer and more like satanic murderer Ricky Kasso. It's an absolute dystopian overdose of ultra-violence, a truly upsetting splatter film in which the plot is secondary to the extreme gore. It's a lot like porn, but with the most disgusting gross-out visuals instead of sex.

You'll be dizzy, sick, stunned, actually disturbed, and genuinely distressed by the extreme gore in *Hobo with a Shotgun*. It's repulsive and not in a guilty pleasure kind of way. It's an overdose of brutal, bleak torture sequences. You'll

worry that it's changing your brain, that it will leave a lasting impact, change your standards for what is acceptable. In this way, the movie is legitimately terrifying. You realize that no matter how the plot resolves, you have been changed by what you have seen.

But this movie is made by a Canadian and set in Canada and so, galdarnit, you're going to stick with it. You stay tuned right to the final line: "You and me are going on a joyride to hell. You're riding shotgun." There's a final hail of bullets as a train whistle blows in the distance. Fade to black. The credits roll to the incongruously peppy '80s synthpop song "Run with Us."

Art makes you feel something, and if you consider "sickened" to be a valid feeling, then *Hobo with a Shotgun* succeeds wildly in an artistic sense. If nothing else, this film dismisses the myth that while Americans might enjoy a boisterous fireworks display after a rowdy parade, Canadians would find it more pleasant to drink tea and quietly crochet an afghan as Peter Mansbridge gently delivers the news on *The National.*

And now I offer this most genteel quiz. A pop quiz? Oh, hush, no, nothing of the sort. Not even a pip quiz. This is just a quiet, mild-mannered, unassuming questionnaire.

1. This movie was made
   a) on a dare
   b) after its trailer won a contest
   c) to fulfill probation requirements
   d) after a bet was lost

2. True or false: *Hobo with a Shotgun* debuted at the Sundance Film Festival.

3. The song "Run with Us" is best known as the theme from which Canadian TV show?
   a) *The Raccoons*
   b) *Danger Bay*
   c) *Ready or Not*
   d) *Max, the 2000-Year-Old Mouse*

4. This film was produced with help from
   a) the company behind award-winning films such as *The Red Violin*
   b) the actor best known as the handsome Mountie Constable Benton Fraser in the television series *Due South*
   c) Film Nova Scotia
   d) the Canadian Film or Video Production Tax Credit
   e) all of the above

ANSWERS

. . . .

1. This movie was made

Answer: b) after its trailer won a contest

So enamoured were American filmmakers Robert Rodriguez and Quentin Tarantino of the exploitation genre's mandate of freedom to include all the baseless gore, nudity, violence, and any other shock-generating footage imaginable that they not only wanted to make an homage to exploitation films, they created a contest to encourage a new generation of filmmakers to be baptized in a splatter of fake blood.

Grindhouse was Rodriguez and Tarantino's contribution to the genre in 2007. It was a cinematic concept comprised of two feature-length movies:

Rodriguez's *Planet Terror* and Tarantino's *Death Proof.* In throwback Hollywood vernacular, a grindhouse is a theatre that shows B-movie fare like exploitation films, often as double features; between movies, trailers for coming attractions are screened. To mirror this format and truly exploit exploitation cinema, Rodriguez and Tarantino ran a contest for emerging filmmakers to produce coming-attractions trailers for fake exploitation movies. The winning entries would be shown during screenings of *Grindhouse.*

Jason Eisener of Dartmouth, Nova Scotia, fresh out of the Screen Arts program at Nova Scotia Community College and still high on the relative success of his debut indie film *Fist of Death*, decided to direct an entry for the competition. Working with producer and Concordia grad Rob Cotterill and writer and

Fist of Death alum John Davies, he created the winning trailer for *Hobo with a Shotgun* in six days.

Even before winning the *Grindhouse* contest, the *Hobo with a Shotgun* trailer became an online sensation in 2007 just as YouTube was emerging as a phenomenon. Fans commented on the video and demanded that a real feature-length film be created. Eisner, Cotterill, and Davies eagerly complied and began working with established feature film producer Niv Fichman of Rhombus Media and *Blade Runner* star Rutger Hauer, who starred as the hobo in the feature-length film.

• • • • • • • • • • • • • • • •

2. True or false: *Hobo with a Shotgun* debuted at the Sundance Film Festival.

Answer: True

Of the 3,812 feature films submitted, *Hobo with a Shotgun* was one of just 118 selected for inclusion at the prestigious American festival. It was scheduled in the Midnight lineup of the program, which is reserved for horror flicks, comedies, and movies that defy genre. It debuted on January 21, 2011, alongside such titles as *Codependent Lesbian Space Alien Seeks Same* and *Trollhunter*.

• • • • • • • • • • • • • • • •

3. The song "Run with Us" is best known as the theme from which Canadian TV show?

Answer: a) *The Raccoons*

"Run with Us" will be familiar to viewers of *The Raccoons*, a trio of early '80s animated Canadian television specials that evolved into a CBC series that aired Sunday nights from 1985 to

1992. Lisa Lougheed, a graduate of the Etobicoke School of the Arts and an alumna of Canada's Wonderland's mascot-filled musical revues, recorded the track and voiced the character of Lisa in the show. The song was released as a single in 1987 and peaked at number eight on RPM's Adult Contemporary chart on January 30, 1988, a week when "Could've Been" by Tiffany held the number one spot.

Lougheed's 1988 debut album, *Evergreen Nights*, was named after the program's Evergreen Forest setting and served as the show's soundtrack. It earned her a 1989 JUNO Award nomination for "Most Promising Female Vocalist of the Year," but Sass Jordan took the prize.

• • • • • • • • • • • • • •

4. This film was produced with help from

Answer: e) all of the above

Hobo with a Shotgun was produced in conjunction with Rhombus Media Ltd., an award-winning film company born in 1978 of the York University film department and known for its work on non-hobo-related fare such as *Thirty Two Short Films About Glenn Gould* and *The Red Violin.*

Canadian actor Paul Gross, who you're for sure picturing in his *Due South* character's RCMP red serge, worked with Whizbang Films from its inception in 1999 until 2012. In that time, the production company helped create the movies *Passchendaele* and *Men with Brooms* in addition to *Hobo with a Shotgun.*

The Nova Scotia Film Industry office, which helped filmmakers secure permits, scout locations, and apply for funding, closed its doors in 2015 after the cash-strapped provincial government reduced the film industry tax credit from 100 percent to just 25 percent. The tax credit had previously helped to ensure the production of those rare successful Canadian shows *This Hour Has 22 Minutes*, *Mr. D*, and *Trailer Park Boys,* and the miniseries *The Book of Negroes.* The Canadian Film or Video Production Tax Credit program still chugs along, doling out tax credits to encourage us to produce Canadian films and videos, no matter how blissful or blood-drenched.

ROUND TWO
Beavers

WHAT'S TRUE AND
WHAT'S A DAM LIE?

5

THE "BEAVER HOUR": CANCON QUOTA GETS A GHETTO SLOT

Radio stations wouldn't touch them. Consumers stayed away in droves. Eventually, the government had to mandate that we hear them. Exactly how bad were the records made in Canada in the 1960s?

Could our nationally produced pop singles possibly have been worse than, say, New Yorker Brian Hyland's 1960 number-one hit "Itsy Bitsy Teenie Weenie Yellow Polka-Dot Bikini"? Surely they weren't as dismal as British band Herman's Hermits' 1965 top hit "'I'm Henery the Eighth, I Am"?

It's good to be Gordon Lightfoot. He's the grinner on the right.

Outside our borders, Canadian-born musicians were recording exceptional material. Neil Young, Joni Mitchell, Leonard Cohen, Gordon Lightfoot, and even pioneering pop idol Paul Anka were throwing down inspired sounds at the dawn of the pop era.

But these musicians recorded, toured, and lived elsewhere, usually in the United States, in order to succeed. What was it about the songs recorded within our borders by our own residents that were so taboo?

In many ways, we will never know how truly terrible the era's national pop output was because it was deemed too awful for radio DJs to play and therefore worthless for bands to invest in recording.

"Few Canadian records are up to the American standard," CKFH's Don Daynard told the *Globe and Mail* in 1968. His colleague, John Donabie, agreed: "I don't want to play third-class records." The station adopted a Top 40 format in 1966 and played one Canadian record a week.

The unlikely prospects for success left Canadian-based bands frustrated. "What can you do when radio stations just aren't interested in Canadian discs?" complained Brian Pombiere, who managed the relatively successful North York, Ontario, one-hit-wonder Lords of London, who had a Canadian hit in 1967 with "Cornflakes and Ice Cream." "We just wouldn't bother to make another disc for the local market;

it's a waste of money, talent, and energy. Forget it," Pombiere told the *Globe* after the band's two follow-up records failed to chart or even garner airplay.

Canadians topped the American *Billboard* chart exactly twice in the 1960s, and these hits offer little explanation of the national prejudice against our own sound. The first was from Toronto bandleader Percy Faith, who had the number one record the week of February 22, 1960, with the languid orchestral theme from the Sandra Dee movie *A Summer Place*. But the track was recorded at the Columbia 30th Street Studio in New York City, and as an instrumental it was very much a holdover from the pre-pop era, when Canadians had had no trouble scoring hits. Just look at bandleader Guy Lombardo of London, Ontario, and his band The Royal Canadians, who sold millions of records worldwide in the big band era between 1927 and 1940. The second and final Canadian number one of the 1960s came from Lorne Greene in 1964. Turns out the Ottawa-born Alpo spokesman and host of *Lorne Greene's New Wilderness* also starred as Pa Cartwright on the American western series *Bonanza*, which ran on NBC from 1959 to 1973. Riding on the strength of these rock-star credentials, Greene released the album *Welcome to The Ponderosa* in 1963 and cut the single "Ringo," backed with the theme from *Bonanza* on the B-side. (In a delightful Canadianism, Greene also recorded a French version of "Ringo," which was backed with "Du Sable.")

"Ringo" was the spoken-word ballad of Old West outlaw Johnny Ringo. It was doubtlessly carried to the number one spot by Beatlemania, which peaked in 1964 and ensured that anything emblazoned or even mildly associated with Ringo Starr was a hot seller.

Are home-based Canadians just not musical? *Pshaw*. In addition to the pre-pop-era success of Guy Lombardo, the Toronto vocal groups the Diamonds, the Crew-Cuts, and the Four Lads produced a combined total of thirty-eight Top 40 *Billboard* hits in the 1950s. Montreal jazz legend Oscar Peterson began a career in 1944 that would culminate in eight Grammy Awards and countless other accolades.

Nova Scotia's homegrown country music superstar Hank Snow began a career in the '50s and became widely recognized as one of the genre's most innovative contributors. But by the end of the 1950s, a lack of investment in emerging technology

Oscar Peterson in 1977.

was leaving Canada behind in the race to the top of the charts. Our few recording studios were outdated compared to those in America and England. "A lot of Canadian records were produced on a real shoestring," *Toronto Star* entertainment reporter Margaret Daly recalled in an interview with CBC Radio's Barbara Frum in 1976. "A bunch of guys would get five hundred dollars together and rent a two-track studio for twelve hours." It didn't take a discriminating audiophile to determine that the results sounded like a low-fi, muddy mess.

It's no wonder promising musicians headed south to record. As Randy Bachman of Winnipeg hit-makers The Guess Who told CBC Radio in 1970, "Originally, we started recording in Minneapolis.... The groups up in Edmonton are even more unfortunate because they drive all the way to New Mexico to record." Guess Who producer Jack Richardson mortgaged his house to raise the $18,000 in capital (about $113,000 in today's dollars) needed for the band to spend five days at A & R Recording Inc., a major studio in New York City. (The gamble paid off — the session spawned the million-selling single "These Eyes.")

Meanwhile, Top 40 radio stations were happy to secure their ratings by following play-list strategies based on *Billboard* charts and proven reports from American programming consultants. Why take a chance on Canadian talent when the current method worked for advertisers, listeners, and broadcasters? "You can't shove Canadianism down people's throats," Garry Ferrier, program director of CHUM Radio, told the *Globe* in 1968.

Pierre Juneau's response was *Just watch me.* The tough-talking, ardent head of the Canadian Radio and Television Commission (CRTC) declared in 1970 that "Canadian broadcasting should be Canadian." Reflecting the brash politics and bold commitments of then prime minister Pierre Trudeau, Juneau introduced strict Canadian content rules for radio and television that came into

Juneau, right, with Trudeau in 1975.

effect in 1971. Canadian content was to comprise 25 percent of playlists. The quota increased to 30 percent in the 1980s and 35 percent in the 1990s.

Private broadcasters were certain that people would turn off their radios if they had to listen to Canadian records.

"The pessimistic view from the broadcasters was that they would lose millions and millions of dollars and they would go out of business," said Daly. "There was no Canadian product that was good enough to play.

Even after the regulations came into effect, the stigma remained.

71

Such was radio stations' determination to keep Canadian content at bay that they resorted to ghettoizing Canadian records and playing them at off-peak hours, typically between 3:00 a.m. and 6:00 a.m., in programming blocks that became known as "Beaver Hours." Think about that: Beaver Hours. Not Skunk Hours or Juneau Hours or CRTC Can Stick It Hours. Beaver Hours. Our broadcasters used a proud national emblem to delineate something they thought was junk. Put it in context by trying to imagine American DJs relegating their least-fave discs to Eagle Hours and the contrast offers a crystal-clear peek into our nation's fragile sense of self-worth.

The CRTC soon closed the Beaver Hours loophole to ensure Canadian content would be heard in prime time. The impact of the ruling was heard immediately: Sam the Record Man, then the country's largest music retailer, reported that Canadian music sales increased 25 percent in 1971. There were thirty-six Canadian singles on the *Billboard* Top 100 charts that year.

Decades later, as records by Canadians from Alanis, Celine, and Shania to Drake, Bieber, and The Weeknd have ruled the charts both at home and abroad, it's easy to reflect on Beaver Hours and wonder: *Did that seriously happen? Is that even real?* Consider, also, these questions:

• • • • • • • • • • • • • •

1. **To help broadcasters identify Canadian music, the CRTC created a classification system that uses which acronym?**
   a) ARSE
   b) MAPL
   c) BEAV
   d) DIRT

2. The CRTC was later forced to amend its classification system because of complaints from

   a) private broadcasters

   b) Bryan Adams

   c) the listening public

   d) Nickelback

3. The annual awards to recognize achievement in Canadian music were renamed the JUNO Awards in 1971 in recognition of Pierre Juneau's contribution to championing Canadian music. What were the awards called prior to this?

   a) The Gold Leaf Awards

   b) The RPM Awards

   c) The Ringos

   d) The Beaver Awards

4. True or False: The CRTC regulates the internet to ensure Canadians surf a minimum of 30 percent Canadian-generated web pages.

5. True or False: In an effort to trick DJs into thinking they weren't Canadian, Canadian music artists and bands often named themselves and their songs after American or European places.

ANSWERS

. . . .

1. To help broadcasters identify Canadian music, the CRTC created a classification system that uses which acronym?

Answer: b) MAPL

In 1970, the CRTC introduced the MAPL system to classify songs. Records generally qualify as "Canadian" if they meet two of these qualifications:

- **M**usic composed entirely by a Canadian
- **A**rtist is Canadian
- **P**roduced in Canada
- **L**yrics written entirely by a Canadian

. . . .

2. The CRTC was later forced to amend its classification system because of complaints from

Answer: b) Bryan Adams

Adams's ballad "(Everything I Do) I Do It for You" hit the top of the charts in seventeen countries, including Canada, in 1991. Although Adams is a Canadian artist, the record didn't qualify under the MAPL system. The album was recorded mostly in England and it was co-written with British record producer Robert John "Mutt" Lange (who was yet to earn the country's scorn by marrying national treasure Shania Twain and then cheating on her with her best friend). Because the record was co-written by a non-Canadian and recorded outside of Canada, the recording met only one qualification of the MAPL system and therefore couldn't be considered Canadian content under CRTC guidelines. Adams, who at the time had already won a dozen of his eighteen JUNO Awards, said the rule was "a disgrace, a shame … stupidity," and called for the abolition of the CRTC. In response, an ad hoc CRTC committee amended the rules so that a Canadian artist who writes 50 percent of a song's music and 50 percent of its lyrics would qualify for a MAPL point.

• • • • • • • • • • • • • • •

3. **The annual awards to recognize achievement in Canadian music were renamed the JUNO Awards in 1971 in recognition of Pierre Juneau's contribution to championing Canadian music. What were the awards called prior to this?**

Answer: a) The Gold Leaf Awards

RPM magazine founded the Gold Leaf Awards in 1970 to honour Canadian music industry achievement. Like the poor sister of America's *Billboard* magazine, *RPM* was the lone Canadian music-industry publication to feature song and album charts for Canada. It was founded by Walt Grealis of Toronto in 1964. In his honour, the JUNOs present the Walt Grealis Special Achievement Award to those who help to advance Canadian music. Still unknown: why the awards are called the JUNOs and not the JUNEAUs. It's not like it would be tricky for the nation to pronounce this surname. The prime minister at the time was named Trudeau, after all.

• • • • • • • • • • • • • • •

4. **True or False: The CRTC regulates the internet to ensure Canadians surf a**

minimum of 30 percent
Canadian-generated web
pages.

Answer: False

They thought about it. They con-
sulted. They deliberated. But in
the end, they decided it wasn't ne-
cessary. "The Canadian new media
industry is vibrant, highly competitive and successful without regu-
lation," announced chairwoman
Françoise Bertrand in 1999.

• • • • • • • • • • • • • • • •

5. True or False: In an effort to
   trick DJs into thinking they
   weren't Canadian, Canadian
   music artists and bands
   often named themselves and
   their songs after American
   or European places.

Answer: False

While there is no evidence to
indicate Canadian musicians

intentionally incorporated the
names of exotic locales to foil
DJs into believing they were
American or European bands,
it's not a huge leap to make that
assumption. Lords of London
likely tried to jump the British
Invasion bandwagon not just
with their name, but also with
their psychedelic sound and
Beatles haircuts. The Irish
Rovers, who scored an unlikely
hit in 1967 with "Unicorn,"
played up their Northern Ireland
homeland even though they all
lived in Canada. Many artists
recorded songs with American
or foreign place names, including Neil Young's hit "Ohio,"
Patsy Gallant's disco foray "New
York to L.A.," The Guess Who's
"American Woman," Anne
Murray's "Tennessee Waltz," R.
Dean Taylor's "Indiana Wants
Me," and Leonard Cohen's
"First We Take Manhattan"

and "Chelsea Hotel #2." But Joni Mitchell is by far the most prolific in this regard. The folk singer heroine of Fort Macleod, Alberta, recorded "Woodstock," "Free Man in Paris," "Chelsea Morning," and "In France They Kiss on Main Street."

HINTERLA
WHO'S W

HINTERLAND
WHO'S WHO

Beaver

6

HINTERLAND WHO'S WHO: COOL FLUTE TUNE BUT BEAVER QUESTIONS REMAIN

To many Canadians, "Flute Poem" is a piece of music as familiar as the *Hockey Night in Canada* theme or "O Canada." While the name of the piece is unfamiliar to most, its sound — like the call of the loon or the bell chimes of a Dickie Dee bike — touches something deep in the recesses of the mind. When we hear the delicate and mournful tune, we know it instantly as the theme of *Hinterland Who's Who*.

The first four installments of the long-running series of wildlife vignettes introduced Canadians

If this is your Milton, Ontario, family availing yourselves of Dickie Dee's services in 1983, please tell your dad his bathing suit is awesome.

to the beaver, the loon, the gannet, and the moose in 1963. The ads aimed for a simple tone that reflected the quiet monotony of nature and were captivating in spite of themselves. From then until 1978, dozens of these seminal TV spots were created and aired with a regularity that falsely assured young viewers that the word *hinterland* was in common use. In fact, the rarely used German term refers to the land behind a city, port, or coast. Likely in service of alliteration, the *Who's Who* gang expanded the definition to include just about anywhere at all that was outside-ish.

Each sixty-second episode of *Hinterland Who's Who* followed the same format. The strains of "Flute Poem" would give way to the low and measured narration of naturalist John Allen Livingston, who would introduce footage of an unassuming, reasonably peaceful-looking wild animal in its natural habitat and then impart one of the many diverse and exciting ways in which our grandparents and great-grandparents had absolutely decimated their numbers.

Each mini-documentary imparted a melancholy little fairy tale about how these creatures died at our hands: The muskox was once brought to near extinction by man and his rifle. Beavers almost disappeared because of overtrapping. The trumpeter swan was overhunted for its plumage. Millions of bison once roamed the prairies until overhunting made them extinct. Human activities caused the population of the roseate tern to decline. The indiscriminate use of insecticides has sharply limited the peregrine falcon's ability to reproduce. The once common swift fox is officially extinct in Canada thanks to poisoning, trapping, and loss of habitat. The cougar was a victim of relentless bounty hunting. Killdeers were routinely kicked in the crotch for their incessant chirping. The ruffed grouse was strangled for fun.

The program became an unintentional way for us to connect with our forefathers in our shared base instinct, which is to look at animals and wonder, *How can this*

Killdeers: not to be kicked.

benefit me? Can I eat it? Ride on it? Pet it? Walk it on a leash? Train it to attack my enemies? Can this creature somehow alleviate the malaise and ennui of my modern life?

Even in noble conservationists, in the back of every mind is the karma-based notion that if I save the beavers, they will thank me. When I need it most, a beaver army will rise up and protect me, or at least they'll let me walk among them like a hoser Jane Goodall. The inherently selfish nature of humans is always lurking somewhere, even behind the best intentions.

In the beaver episode, we learn that "the beaver builds dams because he has to store his winter food in water deep enough not to freeze." What is never resolved is the central mystery of the beaver that is buried deep in its evolutionary biology. Beavers eat twigs, bark, and leaves that are found on land, but beavers are awkward on land, which makes them vulnerable to predators. Instead of undergoing evolutionary modifications that would have either

Might as well keep yourself busy.

changed the beavers' diet to predominantly aquatic plants, which they could access safely through the water, or made the beaver increasingly swift on land so it could maintain its diet but avoid predators, beavers instead stubbornly decided to engage in an inordinate amount of busy-work to build dams that flood the area around trees so they can access them from the water. It's a ridiculous routine of modifying the environment to fit their very specific needs. And it's an approach that all Canadians can identify with as they install their snow tires or virtually bathe in bug spray or don a parka or shovel out their walkways.

Each installment of *Hinterland Who's Who* closed by offering more information to those who wrote to the Canadian Wildlife Service, the agency that produced the ads in conjunction

with the National Film Board. Hundreds of people wrote for wildlife information pamphlets each week, many of them children. It was a generation who learned that they could best interact with wildlife through TV and Canada Post.

The original vignettes of the '60s and '70s continued to appear on TV through the '90s. In 2003, the series was rebooted by the Canadian Wildlife Federation in conjunction with Environment and Climate Change Canada. In the relentlessly cheesy renaissance, the bass drops during "Flute Song," which then morphs into a hip hop audio backdrop for a narrator who appears onscreen to cheerily impart our modern approach to arse-ing up life for our furry and feathered neighbours.

Wildlife footage is largely axed in favour of face time for the host, invariably a chipper young Canadian Wildlife Service worker who is happily invading the animal's natural habitat. In the freshwater turtle installment, the host is actually holding one.

The new installments also update the species' victim narrative to impart not just how our forefathers decimated their population but to enumerate the many ways in which we now offhandedly end these animals. In one typical episode, a perky, ponytailed host appears onscreen, holding a beguiling purple balloon. "See this helium balloon? Harmless enough, right? Well, if a leatherback turtle mistakes balloons for food and eats them, they can get stuck in his intestines, causing the turtle to die." The YouTube subtitles are liberally sprinkled with exclamation points, an item of punctuation foreign to the original narrator.

The reboot videos are offered on YouTube in English and French, with subtitles in Punjabi, Spanish, Mandarin, and Arabic, presumably to welcome Canada's newcomers to the inherent guilt associated with our nation's wildlife. Welcome! No balloons, please.

Doooo-do-do-dooo-dooo-do-do-do-dooooo! (This is the flute song introduction to the quiz portion of this chapter.)

• • • • • • • • • • • • • • •

1. **The National Film Board was created largely to**

    a) help win the Second World War

    b) capture the majesty of the beaver

    c) combat Quebec separatism

    d) make films about hockey

• • • • • • • • • • • • • • • •

2. "Flute Poem" composer John Cacavas also wrote the score for which TV series?

   a) *Kojak*
   b) *Hawaii Five-O*
   c) *The Bionic Woman*
   d) *Buck Rogers in the 25th Century*
   e) all of the above

• • • • • • • • • • • • • • •

3. Original narrator John Allen Livingston went on to become a

   a) legendary environmental educator
   b) popular bluegrass fiddler
   c) roller coaster designer
   d) terrifying murderer

• • • • • • • • • • • • • • • •

4. Which mystery emerged on the occasion of the series's fiftieth anniversary in 2013?

   a) the whereabouts of the original four installments of *Hinterland Who's Who* from 1963
   b) the origin of the invasive species known as the House Hippo
   c) the location of the sheet music for "Flute Poem"
   d) all of the above

ANSWERS

• • • • • • • • • • • • • • •

1. The National Film Board was created largely to

Answer: a) help win the Second World War

The National Film Board was designed to bolster war efforts, but you could easily be forgiven for believing hockey is its raison d'être. A non-exhaustive list of its hockey films includes *Shinny: The Hockey in All of Us*, *Here's Hockey!*, *Blades and Brass*, *Junior*, *The Hockey Sweater*, *Of Sport and Men*, *When Hockey Came to Belfast*, and *Overtime*.

The Canadian government had been in the movie business since establishing the Canadian Government Motion Picture Bureau in 1918. In an early example of government navel-gazing, it commissioned a study into its own film production in the late 1930s. The National Film Board was created in 1939 in response to the study, and it immediately went to work in support of the nation's war effort by cranking out pro-Canada propaganda in the form of *Canada Carries On*, a series of morale-boosting theatrical shorts created thanks in part to financial backing from Canada's Wartime Information Board. The most notable film of the series is 1941's *Churchill's Island*, which won the first-ever Academy Award for Best Documentary (Short Subject). Like many of the 199 films produced in the series before its end in 1959, it was narrated by Ottawa-born actor Lorne Greene.

• • • • • • • • • • • • • • •

2. "Flute Poem" composer John Cacavas also wrote the score for which TV series?

ROUND TWO — BEAVERS

Answer: e) all of the above

The South Dakota–born composer befriended actor Telly Savalas while working in London, England, in the 1970s. This friendship led Cacavas to Hollywood, where he would go on to score *Kojak*, *Hawaii Five-O*, *The Bionic Woman*, *Buck Rogers in the 25th Century*, and the 1972 cult film *Horror Express*. In 2005, Cacavas composed the theme song for the video game *Grand Theft Auto: Liberty City Stories*.

• • • • • • • • • • • • • • •

3. Original narrator John Allen Livingston went on to become a:

Answer: a) legendary environmental educator

Once a producer on *The Nature of Things*, John Allen Livingston went on to become a legendary environmental educator who was a key player in the establishment of York University's Faculty of Environmental Studies. His provocative non-fiction book *Rogue Primate: An Exploration of Human Domestication* won the prestigious Governor General's Award in 1994.

He is not to be confused with Philadelphia-born roller coaster designer John C. Allen, who is credited with popularizing wooden coasters, or with Juno award–winning fiddler John P. Allen, who played in Tommy Hunter's band and was a member of Prairie Oyster.

He is most certainly not to be confused with Anthony John Allen, a British man who faked his own suicide in 1966 and was convicted of a triple murder in 2002.

· · · · · · · · · · · · · · · ·

4. Which mystery emerged on the occasion of the series's fiftieth anniversary in 2013?

Answer: a) the whereabouts of the original four installments of *Hinterland Who's Who* from 1963

It's the ads' low-key, rather boring format that makes it so surprising that they sparked one of the most compelling Canadian mysteries of the 2010s. In a plot worthy of a modern-day *Murdoch Mysteries*, footage of the four original installments from 1963 were missing as the occasion of the series's fiftieth birthday approached.

The archives and storerooms of the Canadian Wildlife Service and the National Film Board were searched with abandon but bore no fruit. The National Archives, too, came up empty. Newspaper headlines cleverly wondered whether the films were hibernating or extinct. It is particularly this kind of conundrum — where the government is a) planning a fiftieth birthday party *for a commercial*, and b) cannot find the commercial — that inspires the wonderment of this book's title.

Annie Langlois, the Ottawa-based Canadian Wildlife Federation's co-ordinator of *Hinterland Who's Who* and chief organizer of the program's fiftieth birthday party, feared that the black and white originals might have been deemed irrelevant with the advent of colour and discarded. In this way, the clips become a metaphor for their subjects: forgotten, taken for granted, eventually hunted down for observation.

The missing instalments were later located by national hero Colin Preston, the library coordinator at the CBC Vancouver media archive. To date, the French-language versions remain missing.

CUCUMBER:
MOOSE + BEAVER + TREE HOUSE
= ZERO CUKES

There is nothing left to be mined from the landscape of late twentieth-century American pop culture. Every last nugget has been extracted from the burrow. There are no commercials, let alone programs, that are forgotten memories still waiting to be unlocked, uncovered, explored, exploited, and examined in self-referential online think pieces. There are no quotes, slang, movements, melodies, or monuments that haven't already been printed on a T-shirt, edited into a GIF, or modelled into a meme.

Case in point is *The More You Know*, NBC's series of family-oriented public service announcements that debuted in 1989. The solemnly earnest segments have featured Betty White espousing the joys of reading, Kelsey Grammer reminding parents to set limits, George Clooney discouraging child abuse, and dozens more.

The sheer number of parodies created in response to the innocuous PSA campaign is, in itself, worthy of parody. *The More You Know* has been referenced in sitcoms like *Will & Grace*, *30 Rock*, *Family Guy*, and *Scrubs*; on late-night talk shows such as *Late Night with Conan O'Brien*, *The Daily Show*, and *The Showbiz Show with David Spade*; on the sketch comedy shows *MADtv* and *Saturday Night Live;* and in the feature film *Penguins of Madagascar.* The online database

GIPHY has more than 28,000 GIFs filed under "The More You Know." Even NBC, the network that created the original ads, produced a cultural callback loop by producing their own parody starring the cast of *Scrubs*.

From Mr. T to the Kool-Aid Man, Americans exchange references to the media, images, and messages of their formative years as a way to relate to one another and build connections. By exchanging these references, they shore up their shared cultural history. But of course Americans do. America is the most sophisticated pop culture generator in the world. Next door in Canada? It's sparse. Canadian media functions to fill in the small spaces available around American content by producing the one thing America doesn't: something inherently "Canadian." And because Canadian content is bound to be diluted in the surrounding swamp waters of American programming, there is an unconscious effort by broadcasters to make Canadian content super-concentrated.

This was certainly the situation in the early 1970s, when then newbie TVO producer Clive VanderBurgh was tasked with creating a new children's show. He found there was a network-based obligation to create an identifiably Canadian show. "I thought, well, if you want to be Canadian, what the heck? Let's go with a moose and a beaver," VanderBurgh recalled in a 2013 interview.

And so it was that, starting in 1974, characters creatively named Moose and Beaver would be the furry, fully costumed hosts of TVO's new live-action children's show with an educational mandate and an unlikely title: *Cucumber* (which stands for Children's Underground Club of United Moose and Beaver for Enthusiastic Reporters). The reporter construct allowed Moose and Beaver to investigate a wide range of curriculum-supporting yet oddly non-cucumber-related topics from their tree house home. They also threw to pre-taped segments featuring real, live children. The show was designed as part of TVO's inaugural block of children's programming to air on Saturday mornings with the station's other in-house children's shows, *Monkey Bars* and *Polka Dot Door*.

In line with the station's mandate to support teachers by creating content that was relevant to school curriculum, VanderBurgh and his colleagues became unexpected pioneers in interactive media. TVO initiated a system in which teachers could call the station to request tapes of *Cucumber* to be delivered to their schools by mail. These tapes could then be played in the classroom to what must have been the most amped students in the world. Maybe you remember the wonder with which you first regarded a Nintendo Wii or the space landing or ordering pizza online or asking Siri for the meaning of life. That's what watching a tape in 1974 in your classroom was like.

In addition, students could mail their artwork and projects to the show to become members of the *Cucumber* Club. Students' work was shown in a regular mail segment on the program in an unlikely incidence of Marshall McLuhan's theory of media as ourselves. Club members received an official button and an issue of *Cucumber* magazine, presumably the repository for Moose and

Beaver's reportage. The button and magazine offer became untenable, as the show, which ended in 1976, was rerun into the '80s, and the TVO budget couldn't cover the ongoing requests. Only two issues of the magazine were produced before it became financially prohibitive.

For all its groundbreaking originality, the obvious similarities between *Cucumber*'s live-action, costumed hosts Moose and Beaver and the famous American moose and squirrel pairing of Rocky and Bullwinkle are undeniable. Moose even talks in a stuffed-up, dopey voice like Bullwinkle. But while Bullwinkle is nude save for his white gloves, Moose wears a varsity pullover emblazoned with an M. Beaver, for her part, has a distinctive outfit of natty yellow-and-red-plaid vest and matching newsboy cap that differentiates her from fellow

bucktoothed rodent Rocket J. "Rocky" Squirrel, whose voice is similar but whose green aviator cap and goggles are distinctly different. Also, Rocky is a flying squirrel and Beaver is a run-of-the-mill Canadian beaver, but she's played by an absolute pro.

In the costume is Nikki Tilroe, whose face you finally saw — albeit covered in white makeup — when she appeared as the Mime Lady on *Today's Special*, which VanderBurgh also created. An Emmy-winning puppeteer, Tilroe operated Muppets on *Fraggle Rock* and was awarded a "Citation of Excellence in the Art of Puppetry" by Jim Henson in 1975. Despite her American roots, she also achieved the Canadian dream: to teach puppetry at the University of Hawaii.

(Even) less well known is the man beneath the moose costume. Alex Laurier was a former *Polka Dot Door* host and a regular musical guest on CFTO's long-running children's show *Uncle Bobby*. After *Cucumber*, he had guest spots on *Seeing Things* and *Street Legal* and appeared in several dinner theatre productions around Toronto. He also taught at the Weist-Barron School of Television, which trained a young Dawn Harrison, who played Cookie on *Kids of Degrassi Street*, whose mom was played by Alannah Myles, who co-wrote a song with MuchMusic VJ Christopher Ward about Elvis (Presley, not Stojko). Their song, "Black Velvet," hit number one on the *Billboard* charts on March 24, 1990, and earned Myles the 1990 Grammy for Best Female Rock Vocalist.

That's a lot of connections. But there can never be enough ways to relate to one another, especially in a place as wide and clumpily populated as Canada. And that is why it's important to rescue *Cucumber* from Canada's cultural wasteland of late-twentieth-century pop culture. Not literally, of course. We're too late for that. All twenty-six episodes and the pilot of the show have been lost. Only the memory and a few brief clips remain.

Now here's something we hope you'll *really* like!

• • • • • • • • • • • • • • •

1. **Who guest-starred on**
    Cucumber?

    a) Prime Minister Pierre Trudeau
    b) Heather Conkie
    c) Martin Short
    d) Liona Boyd

• • • • • • • • • • • • • • •

2. **Wait, why does Heather**
    Conkie's name ring a bell?

    a) she was the host of *Report Canada*
    b) she played the lead role in *Dear Aunt Agnes*
    c) she was on *Polka Dot Door*
    d) she starred in *It's Mainly Music*
    e) all of the above

• • • • • • • • • • • • • • •

3. **Which SCTV alum made his/**
    her TV debut on _Cucumber_?

    a) John Candy
    b) Andrea Martin
    c) Catherine O'Hara
    d) Dave Thomas
    c) all of the above

• • • • • • • • • • • • • • •

4. **Which Canadian musician**
    was profiled on the show as
    a nine-year-old?

    a) Sarah McLachlan
    b) Donna Grantis
    c) Jeff Healy
    d) Melissa Auf der Maur

ANSWERS

. . . .

1. Who guest-starred on Cucumber?

Answer: c) Martin Short

In one of the show's few surviving online clips, Martin Short appeared on the show as Smokey the Hare wearing a rabbit costume which, for some glorious reason, did not cover his face. And while Moose and Beaver's resemblance to Rocky and Bullwinkle is never addressed, it is acknowledged that Smokey the Hare's name is a takeoff on Smokey the Bear. Martin, who would go on to star in *SCTV*, *Saturday Night Live*, and a slew of

Martin Short, centre, flanked by fellow Canadians Paul Shaffer (in round sunglasses) and Eugene Levy (in round not-sunglasses).

shows and movies, sings a melancholy song about ecological destruction that delivers a guilt trip that would put even *Hinterland Who's Who* to shame.

It's worth noting that the instinct by Canadian creators like VanderBurgh to go overboard in the face of network requests to make a show that was created in Canada by Canadians somehow *more Canadian* is exactly what led to the creation of *SCTV*'s franchise-generating skit, "Great White North," in 1980. Its characters, Bob and Doug McKenzie, were created and played by Rick Moranis and Dave Thomas as amalgams of Canadian stereotypes in an effort to appease the CBC's request for CanCon. The sketch's signature "Coo-loo-coo-coo-coo-coo-coo-coo" theme is based on "Flute Song" from *Hinterland Who's Who*. The beer-drinking, toque-wearing

eh-sayers connected with Canadian audiences immediately and their popularity spawned a pair of albums and a hit feature film. Never has there been a nation that so unabashedly revels in its own stereotypes.

Award yourself half a point if you answered Heather Conkie. In the pilot episode of *Cucumber*, Moose and Beaver were joined by two human hosts: Short and Conkie. When TVO picked up the show, VanderBurgh nixed the human hosts in favour of just Moose and Beaver.

Prime Minister Trudeau and classical guitar star Liona Boyd never appeared on the show, but did you know they dated? (They did. For eight years.)

• • • • • • • • • • • • • •

2. Wait, why does Heather Conkie's name ring a bell?

Answer: e) all of the above

Heather Conkie is the queen of Canadian television. Not only did she star in *It's Mainly Music*, TVO's music education program — she also played the role of her landlady, Agnes Peabody, in the series. The landlady character proved so popular that she was spun off into her own series, *Dear Aunt Agnes*.

Report Canada replaced *Report Metric* on TVO in 1978. Conkie hosted both. *Report Metric* helped kids get a handle on the metric system, which Canada was then adopting. *Report Canada* saw Conkie as the anchor of a kid-focused news program that covered history, geography, and society and also featured artwork sent in by viewers.

Conkie, who got her start on *Polka Dot Door*, went on to write for *Heartland*, *Emily of New Moon*, and *Road to Avonlea*, among many other Canadian productions. Fun fact: She guest-starred as a nurse on the low-budget Canadian series *Police Surgeon* in 1972. Other stars who appeared on the show, which was legendarily so cash-strapped that actors had to change wardrobe in the bushes because a trailer would have been a budget-buster, include John Candy, William Shatner, and Leslie Nielsen.

• • • • • • • • • • • • • • • •

3. Which SCTV alum made his/ her TV debut on *Cucumber*?

Answer: a) John Candy

Candy guest-starred as a weatherman in a lost episode of *Cucumber* in which he is reportedly svelte as heck. Andrea Martin made her TV debut in 1971 on *The Hart & Lorne Terrific Hour*, a surrealist CBC show that also starred Toronto-born Lorne Michaels, best known for creating and producing *Saturday Night Live*.

Catherine O'Hara got her start on the long-running comedy program *The Wayne & Shuster Show* in 1975. Dave Thomas appeared as James the security guard on *The David Steinberg Show*, a show about a talk show that conceivably provided the blueprint for *The Larry Sanders Show*.

· · · · · · · · · · · · · · · ·

4. Which Canadian musician was profiled on the show as a nine-year-old?

Answer: c) Jeff Healy

A young Jeff Healy made three separate appearances on *Cucumber*. The pre-taped segments showed the young blind guitarist at his cottage and aimed to help viewers understand the five senses.

Healy was born in 1966, two years before Grammy-winning singer-songwriter Sarah McLachlan came into the world in Halifax, Nova Scotia. Donna Grantis made the semifinals in the North American Jimi Hendrix Electric Guitar Competition when she was just sixteen years old and earned a jazz performance degree from McGill University before joining Prince's band, the New Power Generation. Melissa Auf der Maur was the bass player in Courtney Love's innovative band Hole before joining the Smashing Pumpkins. Neither Auf der Maur nor Grantis has any record of an onscreen encounter with Moose and Beaver although McLachlan has shared the screen with rescue dogs.

THE BEAVER:
TITTERING PERVS FORCE
MAG'S NAME CHANGE

It's hard to conceptualize just how long ago 1920 was. Truly, if you can remember it, you weren't really there. It was the year our now-seemingly ancient entities were just coming into their own: the Catholic Women's League was established in Montreal, the Group of Seven unveiled its first exhibition in Toronto, and out west, the Royal Canadian Mounted Police was formed from the North-West Mounted Police. The Bay celebrated an anniversary that year, and it wasn't their fifth or even their fiftieth: it was the 250th anniversary of the Hudson's Bay Company, an astonishing accomplishment for one of the world's oldest brands.

Yes, The Bay, the store that anchors your aging mall, the place you pop in to to grab a stash of red Olympics mittens for stocking stuffers and where you peruse the clothing and footwear while considering the price in the context of the "comparable at" tags at Winners. That very shop — well, not that very shop, as

those bricks and mortar were likely a product of the mall-building craze of the '70s and '80s — but that brand, The Bay, is older than Jean Chrétien, older than Lloyd Robertson, older even than our nation.

The Bay's 250th birthday was marked in 1920 with grand parties, an elaborate ceremonial flotilla, and a specially commissioned bronze anniversary medal. The least-sexy element of the celebration was the establishment of a corporate newsletter. Its

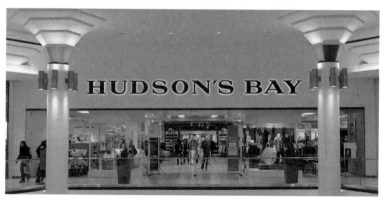

This very shop(-ish).

October launch positioned it as almost an afterthought.

The Bay newsletter's name was determined through a countrywide competition for employees. Picture in your head the contest entrants who scribbled a naughty double entendre on their entry form and popped it in the post box as they snickered to themselves. Now picture their gleeful disbelief when the official name of the newsletter was announced and the name they'd facetiously suggested became official. The dignified publication primly unveiled in celebration of a national institution's great and heralded milestone would be known as *The Beaver.*

The etymology of the word *beaver* as it relates to a woman's "down there" area predates the establishment of The Bay's newsletter and is possibly older than the Hudson's Bay Company itself. While amateur linguists suggest that lady parts earned this nickname because of their visual similarity to beaver fur, this book would be doing a disservice if it did not find a way to delicately relay that it is not because of a hairy similarity that the nickname was created, but because — now clutch your pearls and reach for your smelling salts — *both eat wood.*

Either the corporate team at the helm of the naming contest was so blinded by pride in their company, which once controlled much of Canada's landmass and owed its initial success to the beaver pelt trade, or they were completely unaware of the double meaning. A third option, that they were in on the joke, seems unlikely in light of the publication's earnest content.

The first issue's cover featured a black and white portrait of Hudson's Bay Company governor Robert Molesworth Kindersley.

He neither smiles nor faces the camera. Inside, there are tales of trappers alongside flattering profiles of urban middle managers interspersed with jokes and poetry, all liberally sprinkled with the jaw-dropping casual racism typical of the era. Five thousand copies of the first issue were distributed, at a cost of $570. And readers laughed at the name.

Starting in 1923, the corporate newsletter was redesigned as a consumer magazine and made available to the general public. Subscriptions cost one dollar (about $14 in today's money). And readers laughed at the name.

The publication nearly folded in 1932 due to the Great Depression, but The Bay's governor appointed a new editor who redesigned the magazine with a focus on photos to make it more visually appealing, in the vein of the then highly successful American magazine *Life*. In retrospect, maybe they took a page out of the wrong American magazine. Considering the enduring success of the racy rag *Cosmopolitan*, one wonders what a wild triumph The Bay could have had on its hands had it just leaned into its suggestive title. Instead, The Bay doubled down on its mandate to "include the whole field of travel, exploration and the trade in the Canadian North as well as the current activities and historical background of the Hudson's Bay Company and all its departments throughout Canada." Fur trade department employees were actually trained in photography to help them capture compelling photos of the north for *The Beaver*'s pages. And readers laughed at the name.

In 1934, novelist Robert Watson became the magazine's new editor and took the magazine in a new, literary direction that was a true departure from its corporate cheerleading origins. And readers laughed at the name.

For the next seventy-five years, the magazine delivered stunning photos and enlightening, beautifully written stories that illuminated for all Canadians the variety, versatility, and vivaciousness of life across this vast land. And readers laughed at the name.

In 1994, the Hudson's Bay Company established Canada's National History Society, which took over publication of the magazine. The society conducted a readers' survey to see if a name change was in order. It wasn't. And so tittering perverts across the land continued to laugh about *The Beaver*'s name until 2010, when a name change was finally announced. But even then, after our increasingly urbane national psyche had grown up through the decades by weathering salacious sex scandals

like the Munsinger Affair, exotic hearsay about Margaret Trudeau and the Rolling Stones, and the provocative visual of David Suzuki on the cover of *StarWeek*, nude but for a fig leaf, the publishers were coy about the reason for the name change.

"I can't tell you how many people, especially kids, called us for information about the rodent for their science project," Deborah Morrison, president of Canada's National Historical Society, told CBC News in 2010. If this confusion were truly the reason to rebrand a historic publication, then surely magazines *The Walrus* and *Owl* are facing a similar volume of erroneous calls and will soon follow suit.

There were reports that internet spam and smut filters, especially those employed by school boards, were erroneously blocking students and other would-be readers from the magazine's online content. But later investigations noted that these filters failed to restrict the results of even the most overt searches, such as "porn" and "naked sex."

"We've become a multi-platform magazine," editor Mark Reid told *Maclean's* in 2010. "It's a historic creature, it's on our nickel, it's a proud part of the fur trade. But in the 21st century, if you are going to rebrand your entire organization, including all that you do, *beaver* is probably not going to be the word that best speaks to what you do, if you know what I mean." Oh, Mr. Reid, what we wouldn't do to get you just to tell us exactly what you mean.

For nearly two years, beginning in 2008, *The Beaver's* twenty-four editorial and board members undertook market research studies and delivered a direct-mail campaign in an effort to choose the magazine's new moniker. Presumably, they tiptoed among what linguists have estimated to be our language's nine-hundred synonyms for vagina and five hundred for penis. If you consider that every word is perverted if you pervert it, you'll never think of, say, a canoe or a hockey stick in the same way again.

In the end, they landed on *Canada's History*, which sounds more like a threat than an editorial mandate. The whole situation raises a lot of questions, not least of which are these:

• • • • • • • • • • • • • • •

1. *Canada's History* (née: *The Beaver*) is Canada's second-oldest magazine; which magazine is the oldest?
    a) *Canadian Living*
    b) *The Hockey News*
    c) *Maclean's*
    d) *Vagina*

2. *Beaver* can also refer to

   a) the main character on a '50s-era American sitcom
   b) a pair of characters in C.S. Lewis's famed series of books
   c) the London School of Economics student newspaper
   d) a boy scout between the ages of five and seven
   e) all of the above

3. As of 2013, *The Beaver/ Canada's History* had a readership of approximately

   a) 350,000
   b) 150,000
   c) 50,000
   d) 10,500

4. *The Beaver*'s name change attracted international media attention in 2010. Match the euphemism-laden reporting to the news outlet:

a) "*The Beaver* is changing its name because of its unintended sexual connotation."	i) Masthead
b) "People have made naughty jokes about *The Beaver* moniker over the decades."	ii) *Globe and Mail*
c) "The reason … is to reflect changes in the content of the magazine as well as clear up any misconceptions."	iii) Reuters
d) "The vast majority of people associate *The Beaver* with … well, you know."	iv) Gadling
e) "The title was doomed by a vulgar alternative meaning …"	v) *New York Times*

ANSWERS

. . . .

1. *Canada's History* (née: *The Beaver*) is Canada's second-oldest magazine; which magazine is the oldest?

Answer: c) *Maclean's*

Maclean's was established in 1905, but has undergone several name changes since its founding. It was first printed in October 1905 under the title *The Business Magazine.* Doubtless because of the sexual connotations of giving someone "the business," it was renamed *The Busy Man's Magazine* just two months later. Obviously, due to the explicit sexual overtones of "the busy man," the magazine was renamed in 1911 in honour of its publisher, Lieutenant-Colonel John Bayne Maclean. Maclean founded a number of Canadian magazines throughout his storied publishing career, including the *Financial Post* in 1907 and *Chatelaine* in 1928.

The Hockey News was founded in 1947 by Ken McKenzie and Will Côté. In 1975, *Canadian Living* magazine was created with financial backing from Labatt's. The American publication *Vagina* was founded in 2011 and eagerly accepts submissions.

. . . .

2. *Beaver* can also refer to

Answer: e) all of the above

The ironically wholesome program *Leave It to Beaver* debuted in 1957 on CBS. Its title referred to main character Theodore "The Beaver" Cleaver. The characters Mr. and Mrs. Beaver appeared in C.S. Lewis's famous series of children's stories, The Chronicles

The *Leave It to Beaver* episode "Beaver's First Date" looks like quite a wild ride.

of Narnia. Along with the weekly newspapers in Oakville and Napanee, Ontario, the London School of Economics student newspaper is called *The Beaver*. Scouts Canada welcomes boys aged five to seven to find fun and friendship in the Beaver Scouts program. No girls or double entendres allowed.

. . . .

3. As of 2013, *The Beaver/Canada's History* had a readership of approximately

Answer: a) 350,000

Surely 350,000 readers can't be wrong: *Canada's History* is delightful, interesting, and worthy of study (much like its former moniker).

. . . .

4. *The Beaver*'s name change attracted international media attention in 2010. Match the euphemism-laden reporting to the news outlet:

Answers:

a) iii) Reuters, the international news agency headquartered in London, England, reported in a typically restrained British way that "*The Beaver* is changing its name because of its unintended sexual connotation."

b) ii) The *Globe and Mail*, a Toronto-based newspaper presumably written *by* adults *for* adults, primly issued this scolding in the year of our Lord 2010: "People have made naughty jokes about *The Beaver* moniker over the decades." You can practically hear the yardstick smacking against your school desk as the word *naughty* is spat out.

c) i) Masthead, which reports on Canada's magazine industry, blithely announced, "The reason …
is to reflect changes in the content of the magazine as well as clear up any misconceptions."

d) iv) Gadling, a popular travel site, took the "wink, wink, nudge, nudge" approach by writing that "The vast majority of people associate *The Beaver* with … well, you know."

e) v) *The New York Times* reported, "The title was doomed by a vulgar alternative meaning …" *The New York Times* style guide, which helps its reporters navigate how to report on obscenities, among other things, states that "readers should not be left uninformed or baffled about the nature of a significant controversy." Presumably, *The Beaver* name change did not fall into the territory of significant controversy.

ROUND THREE
Hip Hop

ARE ANY OF THESE
SCENARIOS LEGIT?

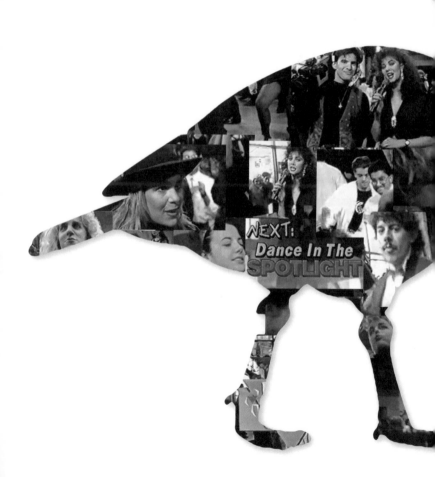

9

ELECTRIC CIRCUS:
LET'S SPANDEX-DANCE
ON TV

Overlooking the Toronto sky-line, this is Toronto Television, Citytv channel 57, cable 7. Everywhere …

A camera pans the exterior of 299 Queen Street West, Toronto's well-known Citytv building. We see a few tourists and passersby looking mildly through the many windows into the first-floor studio where Dini Petty tapes *CityLine*, the same spot from which *Breakfast Television* is broadcast.

It is daylight. It's not dramatically, suddenly daybreak or anything that spectacular. It's just a regular sunny Saturday, mid-afternoon — a civil hour at which most respectable people would be awake, sober, and probably not dancing about.

Cue dance music.

The camera takes us inside the building and into the *CityLine* studio, except there's no Dini Petty, the stage is gone, and there's no sign of the audience bleachers. Instead, people are dancing. On the floor. Up on risers. All over. They are conspicuously dancing. But it's the dance equivalent of a fake smile: there is no smize in their step, just a repetitious, self-conscious, step-touch-clap, step-touch-clap. This is the half-arsed daytime dancing of 1980s Canadians. This is *Electric Circus.*

The women are styled like their icon, pop star Debbie Gibson. Their frosted highlights are permed, their bangs are teased high, their glorious manes are pulled into French braids or they erupt from scrunchy-bound ponytails. Dazzling dangling earrings brush against blush-streaked cheeks. On the men, there is hockey hair, Cosby sweaters, and pleated pants. At least one wears a bolo tie.

The hosts appear on camera. On the left, a heavily-moussed George Lagogianes with a full face of contouring makeup wears a turtleneck and vest. On his shoulder is propped the ever-present video camera. *But if he is shooting the show, who is shooting him? Will Lagogianes ever shoot the second shooter?* The Citytv hand-held camera videographer paradox is the Canadian equivalent of America's JFK assassination second-shooter theory.

Beside him, Monika Deol stands slick with a mic in her hands. "Hi, and welcome to the *Electric Circus.*" She turns to her co-host. "George, how's it going?"

Debbie Gibson: The American Alanis.

"Great." Too long of a pause follows, just one of the many anxious indicators that this is live TV. "It's … it's going just wonderfully. Except it's too cold again." This is the most popular epitaph in Canada.

Deol wisely ignores him and slides right into an announcement for a city-wide dance competition before throwing to a Neneh Cherry video, which is interspersed with shots of dancers live in the studio.

The *Electric Circus* program, which debuted on Citytv in 1988, was designed as a live dance music program in the vein of U.S. fare like *American Bandstand* and *Soul Train*. Like its precursor, Citytv's own '70s disco escapade, *Boogie*, it incorporated stilted hosting, fashion victims, unfortunate hairdos, and questionable dance moves into a *fest du fromage* that careened around a budget set to the hottest sounds of the day. In short, *Electric Circus* was born into the media landscape as a fully formed awkward preteen. It's almost as though visionary network head Moses Znaimer had planned it that way.

Six months after Znaimer ambitiously founded Citytv in 1972, he told a businessmen's luncheon, "We have three production techniques. We have poverty. We have inexperience. And we have fear." The poverty technique, at least, was still in play more than fifteen years later.

"The budget of the show was mostly below the line," recalled producer Joel Goldberg in an interview with *Vice*. "At the beginning it was very tough because people would laugh at us, like, 'What's this stupid dance show?'" Host Monica Deol echoed the sentiment, "Most people in the station thought we were a joke and we were a little bit cheesy."

Although the dancers on *Electric Circus* are in their late teens and twenties, you can easily imagine they're trapped at a middle school dance in hell. Sure, people like to dance with their friends, but dancing with your friends in a circle for ninety minutes in a hot, brightly lit studio with no bar, no food, no seating, no segue into socializing, and with the dual audience of bemused Queen Street bystanders and video cameras broadcasting you live across the country, it's hard to fathom the participants' motivation. There's not a strong market for go-go dancers in Toronto, but surely if this were a career path one wanted to pursue, there would be less-ridiculous routes to success than appearing for free on a Canadian afternoon dance show.

From inside the building, the camera produces a different perspective on the sparse crowd on Queen Street who are looking in on the scene through the windows. We, the home viewers, now know what they're looking at. But their faces show that they're not quite sure what to make of what they're seeing. And even though entrance to the studio is free and open to the public and they could walk just mere paces to the door and enter this spectacle at least to take a closer look, they don't. They prefer to watch this from a distance. Not the level of distance provided by their TVs at home, mind you. Just window distance.

For five years, *Electric Circus* awkwardly shuffled along, alternating between music videos and live shots of dancers in the studio. Across the country, we watched the videos and watched the dancers in the studio watch the videos and watched Lagogianes cut from shooting himself in a mirror to shooting the dancers in the studio watching the videos and watching the video Lagogianes has shot of the dancers in the studio watching the video, on and on in a nested image looping infinitely, a self-referential entertainment system of instancing that recurses on and on into the abyss only to be abruptly interrupted by Hostess potato chip commercials, because when you've got the munchies, nothing else will do.

But then, in 1993, everything changed. *Electric Circus* was moved from Citytv to its sister station, MuchMusic, a natural evolution for a show that heavily featured music videos. But more significant was that the program's time slot shifted to the evening. The show switched from airing a mix of rock, pop, and dance videos to a diet of underground, emerging techno, and house sounds from EDM hotspots like Detroit, Chicago, and Europe. Serious club kids now swung by the *Electric Circus* studio to warm up before a night out at underground raves in the city's burgeoning dance scene.

Electric Circus, the plucky, dorky show that wouldn't quit, had emerged from an extended puberty an absolute stunner, finally ready to bust moves and break curfew.

The windows remained part of the show, but now they were flung open — even in the depths of winter — and dancers stationed on risers acted as funky billboards to the entranced passersby. Now fans lined up along Queen Street for a chance to get inside, where effervescent dancers in shiny pleather and zebra print vogued and mugged for the camera. "Even on a day when it was -30, we still had the windows open and people would be standing out there," recalls producer Sharon Kavanaugh.

The documentary series *Rough Cuts* featured *Electric Circus* in an episode that was shown abroad and that helped the show attract an international following. Producers from MTV came to take notes. Will Smith came by when he was in town. The show featured appearances by the era's biggest names, including Britney Spears, Pink, Snoop Doggy Dogg, Puff Daddy, Destiny's Child, and many more.

But *Electric Circus*'s biggest legacy is the attention it paid to DJs. The show lavished airtime on live guest DJs like Freaky Flow, MC Flipside, and David Morales, and profiled them with a reverence on par with that

afforded to rock stars, helping to establish the now-omnipresent cult of the DJ as celebrity. The show had hit its stride just in time for rave culture to enter the mainstream and electronica to emerge as a major music-label buzzword, with everyone from Madonna to The Tea Party jumping on the trend.

It's going just wonderfully, indeed. Never mind that it is too cold again. Luckily, nothing warms the cockles of one's heart like a good quiz:

• • • • • • • • • • • • • • •

1. **The *Electric Circus* TV show took its name from**
   a) a nightclub
   b) a heavy metal album
   c) a British children's show
   d) a Japanese garage rock song

2. **Leonard Cohen described Citytv co-founder Moses Znaimer as**
   a) the CPR of music
   b) the FBI of music
   c) the CSI of music
   d) the BFF of music

3. **No, that's not a typo — Dini Petty hosted *CityLine* prior to Marilyn Denis's nineteen-year run, which led into Tracy Moore's turn at the helm. What business is Dini Petty in now?**
   a) kitty litter
   b) city litter
   c) kitty Twitter
   d) Twitter pity
   e) broadcasting

4. **The first video aired on MuchMusic was**
   a) "Video Killed the Radio Star" by the Buggles
   b) "The Enemy Within" by Rush
   c) "Somethin' on My Mind" by Teenage Head
   d) "The Kid Is Hot Tonite" by Loverboy

Answers

• • • • • • • • • • • • • • • •

1. The *Electric Circus* TV show took its name from

Answer: a) a nightclub

The show's namesake is a defunct nightclub. Prior to moving to 299 Queen Street West in 1987, the Citytv studios were located at 99 Queen Street East. And prior to Citytv occupying that space, it was the Electric Circus nightclub (and before that, it was a chocolate factory). Electric Circus was opened with much fanfare in 1968 by impresario Stan Freeman, who declared Toronto to be "one of the grooviest cities in the world for rock" and set about importing all the bananas elements of his flagship New York City club to ensure that the town could live up to his proclamation. Among the club's woefully ahead-of-its-time elements were computer-driven strobe lights, foam, EDM, and a merch shop.

The club's VIP opening night party was attended by local luminaries, including Eaton's department store heir John Craig Eaton II, Clairtone stereo inventor Peter Munk, and dope-ass communication theorist and celebrity intellectual Marshall McLuhan. Invited guest Prime Minister Pierre Trudeau was a no-show.

The nightclub was intended to offer an anything-goes mixed-media pleasure dome of light shows, music, circus performers and experimental theatre in which guests could tune in and turn on after paying their $4 cover charge. And it sounds like a pretty sweet deal until your Google-aided calculations reveal that four dollars in 1968 is worth a whopping twenty-eight dollars today.

Beyond the challenge of providing value to patrons in exchange for the steep cover, the club struggled with creditors, incomplete renovations, and internal management discord. In the end, it failed to find its niche and closed in 1970.

Citytv, which had been granted a broadcast licence by the CRTC in 1971, renovated the building and first went on air from the studios at 99 Queen Street East in 1972.

Don't be too hard on yourself if you missed this answer. Electric Circus was also a segment on the '90s BBC children's show *Live & Kicking* and a 2003 single from the Japanese garage rock band Thee Michelle Gun Elephant. And *Inside the Electric Circus* is the title of the 1986 album from Los Angeles heavy metal band W.A.S.P. But that's not what the *Electric Circus* TV show was named after.

· · · · · · · · · · · · · · ·

2. Leonard Cohen described Citytv co-founder Moses Znaimer as:

Answer: a) the CPR of music

Leonard Cohen, whom Moses Znaimer inducted into the Canadian Music Hall of Fame at the 1991 JUNO Awards, described the media mogul as "the CPR of music." It's a fitting tribute to Znaimer, who brought many music-based shows to air, such as *Boogie*, *Stevedore Steve's Big Time City Slickers*, and *People Who Sing Together*, not to mention the groundbreaking weekly newsmagazine program *The NewMusic*, which ran from 1979 to 2008. Znaimer, who now heads ZoomerMedia, co-created MuchMusic, Canada's 24-hour music video station. Its 1984 launch helped connect Canadian music to the youth market and held the ever-encroaching American media, this time in the form of MTV, at bay.

· · · · · · · · · · · · · · · ·

3. No, that's not a typo — Dini Petty hosted *CityLine* prior to Marilyn Denis's nineteen-year run, which led into Tracy Moore's turn at the helm. What business is Dini Petty in now?

Answer: a) kitty litter

Now seventy-two, the veteran broadcaster, successful entrepreneur, and pioneering traffic reporter and helicopter pilot is enjoying retirement, but keeps busy with new business ventures. In 2016, she launched a Kickstarter campaign to help relaunch the three-tray, scoop-free Luuup litter box system.

· · · · · · · · · · · · · · · ·

4. The first video aired on MuchMusic was

Answer: b) "The Enemy Within" by Rush

Give yourself a point if you answered correctly. When "the nation's music station" launched on August 31, 1984, VJs J.D Roberts and Christopher Ward played the epic Toronto prog-rock trio first. Lose a point if you answered "Video Killed the Radio Star." You confused the nations' music stations: the Buggles were the first band played on MTV when it launched on August 1, 1981.

10

MAESTRO FRESH-WES: THE BACKBONE OF CANADIAN HIP HOP

Each music genre has its own menu of cultural signifiers to choose from for music video visuals. These clues help viewers determine what kind of music they're watching. For example, the country music menu is heavy on farm fields, pickup trucks, dogs, beer, cowboy hats, white girls in sundresses, hay bales, jeans, sweat, and smiles. For '80s hair metal, it was guitar solo close-ups of facial grimaces, long-legged white women in stiletto heels, sports cars, lead-singer mic-stand grabs, tight pants,

permed hair, cigarettes, motor-
cycles, and leather. The hip hop
bill of fare includes party people
in the house, graffiti, break dancing, matching jumpsuits, train-
ers, necklaces, turntables, and the
shaking of multicultural booty.

Rapper Maestro Fresh-Wes's
1989 video for "Let Your
Backbone Slide" hit on a meaning-
ful melange of hip hop symbolism.
It was a champagne cocktail of
records spinning, hands in the air
carelessly waving, breakbeat back-
flips, backwards ball caps, braids,
Hammer pants, brass knuckles,
and absolute funky grooving.
The entire production looked
exquisitely American, which is to
say, eminently professional. Even
though it was homegrown and
directed by *Electric Circus* producer Joel Goldberg, there was no
way for international audiences to
know this was a Canadian export.
It was just that good.

Many Canadians were excit-
ed. "Yes, yes!" we hissed under
our breath, cheering him on. *He
hadn't tipped his hand.* There were
no awkward moose walk-ons in
the video. He didn't rhyme anything with Etobicoke or Regina.
The Canadian flag didn't make a
cameo appearance. This boy had
big talent and the added magical
factor that no one could tell he
was Canadian. *Godspeed, young
blood. You might actually make it.*

And he did. In 1989, the success of "Let Your Backbone Slide"
made Maestro Fresh-Wes the
first Canadian rapper in history
to have an American Top 40 hit.
It was certified gold for selling
more than 50,000 copies and was
the bestselling Canadian hip hop
single for twenty-one years until
Kardinal Offishall's "Dangerous"
and K'Naan's "Wavin' Flag" in
2010. The success of "Let Your
Backbone Slide" led directly

K'Naan rocks it at Montreal's Osheaga Festival in 2010.

to the creation of the Best Rap Recording category starting at the 1991 JUNO Awards, which Maestro Fresh-Wes won for his album *Symphony in Effect*. His breakout success led to tour dates with American rap heavy-hitters Public Enemy.

Born Wes Williams in 1968 to Guyanese immigrants in Toronto, Maestro Fresh-Wes had absolutely gone beyond, risen above, cut across. The Maestro had transcended.

Prior to Wikipedia's launch in 2001, there was no easy, go-to reference to find out the nationality of your favourite star, and some Americans in the pre-internet era were dismayed to learn that many of the biggest celebrities of the day — including Jim Carrey,

Michael J. Fox, Mike Myers, Pamela Anderson, Matthew Perry, Jason Priestly, Alanis Morissette, and Celine Dion — were actually Canadian. A 1997 broadcast of the long-running Chicago-based radio show *This American Life* unveiled the shock and discomfort Americans felt when they were told that many — so many — of the people at the epicentre of American culture were Canadian. The most outrageous reaction was reserved for the anchor of *ABC World News Tonight*, Toronto-born Peter Jennings. "I can't believe it," said Peabody-winning *This American Life* producer Alix Spiegel. "He delivers information about America to Americans. He interprets our culture for us. It's like having some Czechoslovakian as your vice president. It's just wrong." So wrong, she thought, that there should be an actual law against it. Spiegel described

the revelation of the celebrities' Canadian nationality as disturbing and spooky to Americans. "It's the invasion of the body snatchers syndrome: they look like us, but they're not us."

Spookily or not, and almost certainly unintentionally, Maestro was passing as an American. He released two successful albums from Canada: 1989's *Symphony in Effect*, which spawned his signature hit with the slick video, "Let Your Backbone Slide," and 1991's *The Black Tie Affair*, with the catchy chart climber "Conductin' Thangs," plus "Nothin' at All," which raised the issue of racism against Aboriginal and Black Canadians. Then Maestro decamped to New York City, using the rightful argument that Canadian media, particularly radio, didn't support rap artists. In 1994, he blew any cover he might have inadvertently been knitting with release of his fourth album, *Naaah, Dis Kid Can't Be from Canada?!!*

Whether it was due to too much punctuation, an overdose of A's, or the sudden, unwelcome revelation that this hip hop star was an interloper from the north, the album was a flop. And the thud the record made when it hit shop shelves resonated in a way that paved the road for the prodigal son to return home.

When Maestro moved back to Canada, it was though a switch had been flipped. In a live 2012 appearance with Public Enemy, he rapped about Rob Ford, Stephen Harper, and even rhymed on René Lévesque. He pulled in fellow Canadian hip hop and rap stars for his epic 2013 album *Orchestrated Noise*, including Kardinal Offishall, Saukrates, Classified, King Reign, Adam Bomb, and E.D.G.E. And

Maestro Fresh-Wes on stage with Nova Scotia rapper Classified at the 2011 JUNO Awards.

he went one further by crossing genre boundaries and inviting Montreal singer-songwriter Sam Roberts and Nova Scotia hard rockers The Trews in on a record that also sampled classic Canadian songs like the Guess Who's "These Eyes" and Blue Rodeo's "Try." It was his biggest success since his debut, even if it left producers befuddled by which cultural signifiers to include in the accompanying music videos.

In press interviews, Maestro is markedly humble, even for a Canadian. And he's extraordinarily humble considering his talent — although to dismiss it as just talent risks discounting the years he spent carefully honing his mad skills.

Maestro grew up in a North York apartment with a musical family. He learned to play piano and was transfixed when his father brought home a 1979 album by New Jersey–based hip hop pioneers The Sugarhill Gang. It inspired him to practise rapping through high school. Later, he worked in a Toronto mall, where he was quite taken by the looks on offer from Ontario mall mainstay and prom rental go-to Tuxedo Royale. The tux look

inspired his maestro style, and his rhymes got him noticed by '80s American Hi-NRG dance-music star Stevie B after Maestro showcased his skills on *Electric Circus*.

Musical conductors direct performances, but when Maestro Fresh-Wes is conductin' thangs, he's doing it more in the sense of an electrical conductor: he's the mechanism through which energy flows and is shared. When asked his advice to aspiring artists, he says, "Don't make records. Make history."

In that spirit, you're invited not just to take this quiz, but to be worthy yourself of becoming quiz fodder.

1. In 2005, Maestro sampled
    a) Lawrence Gowan's "A Criminal Mind"
    b) Kim Mitchell's "Go for Soda"
    c) Loverboy's "Working for the Weekend"
    d) Platinum Blonde's "Crying Over You"

2. True or false: Maestro's move to the States invited scholarly commentary in Canada.

3. Which personalities have been inducted into the Scarborough Walk of Fame?
    a) Lawrence Gowan
    b) Deborah Cox
    c) Marilyn Denis
    d) Maestro
    e) all of the above

4. Which *Canadian Idol* judge got his/her start as Maestro's manager?
    a) Farley Flex
    b) Zack Werner
    c) Sass Jordan
    d) Jake Gold

ANSWERS

. . . .
1. In 2005, Maestro sampled

Answer: a) Lawrence Gowan's "A Criminal Mind"

Lawrence Gowan appears in the video for Maestro's take on Gowan's hit "A Criminal Mind," and his vocals are sampled on the track. The pair performed the song together live at the 2006 Canadian Urban Music Awards.

. . . .
2. True or false: Maestro's move to the States invited scholarly commentary in Canada.

Answer: true

Dr. Rinaldo Walcott is the associate professor and chair of the Department of Sociology and Equity Studies at the Ontario Institute for Studies in Education at the University of Toronto (or, as the cool kids call it, SESE at OISE at U of T). He wrote about Maestro's lyrics and his move from Canada to New York in his 1997 book, *Black Like Who?*, which drew on his PhD research into rap music and culture.

. . . .
3. Which personalities have been inducted into the Scarborough Walk of Fame?

Answer: e) all of the above

Yes, the Scarborough Walk of Fame is a thing that exists separately and beyond the Hollywood Walk of Fame or even Canada's Walk of Fame. Lawrence Gowan, the JUNO-winning solo hit maker and current member of the band Styx, was inducted in 2011. R & B powerhouse Deborah Cox, who, like Whitney Houston, was discovered by famed Arista Records president Clive Davis, was inducted in 2008. Broadcasting legend and long-time TV and radio host Marilyn Denis of *CityLine* and CHUM FM's morning show, *Roger, Rick & Marilyn*, was inducted in 2009. Wesley Williams, alias Maestro Fresh-Wes, was a member of the inaugural induction cohort in 2006.

• • • • • • • • • • • • • • •

4. Which *Canadian Idol* judge got his/her start as Maestro's manager?

Answer: a) Farley Flex

Flex, the son of Trinidadian immigrants, managed the career of Maestro Fresh-Wes at a time when there was barely a daydream, let alone a blueprint, for a successful career in Canadian rap.

He was later instrumental in the launching of Canada's first black-owned-and-operated radio station, which didn't come to fruition until 2000, a full twelve years after Flex and his colleagues had started petitioning the CRTC for a licence for Flow 93.5 FM. "The CRTC has historically licensed on language not culture," Flex told the *Trinidad and Tobago Guardian* in 2015. "Unfortunately, because the lion's share of people of African descent speak English, we fell into a larger group of [English-speakers].... The governing body should license by culture, because our culture is distinctly different [from] other English-speaking communities," he explained. Flex led three campaigns to convince the CRTC before he found success. With that hurdle cleared, he and his team set their sights on television. First Entertainment Voice of Africa TV (FEVA TV) shows black television programming and films from Africa, the States, the U.K., Canada, and the Caribbean.

SNOW: ALL THE "INFORMER" INFO THAT'S FIT TO PRINT

In 1993, discussions of cultural misappropriation and racial stereotyping weren't as finely tuned as they are today. A review of Google Trends shows that the phrase "cultural appropriation" didn't really emerge as a popular label for an ongoing social issue until 2013.

While the early '90s is certainly within the era of political correctness, society was then (as always) often unaware of how properly to do unto others as you would have them do unto you — or it was unwilling to do so.

Now, thanks to social media,

we can easily tweet a response to Macklemore's critique of Miley Cyrus and Iggy Azalea's white privilege. But twenty-plus years ago, without the ability to monitor friends, colleagues, and fellow citizens closely via the digital recording and dissemination technology of today, there were far fewer chances to helpfully correct or properly pillory members of the public.

There were no cellphones to film the occasional, mostly innocent mild transgressions and no internet on which to share them. Casual comments generally weren't considered egregious enough to warrant an article in the newspaper. And if it was on TV, so what? People would watch it and then it would be over. This kind of thing wasn't worth setting the VCR for. No need to get your knickers in a twist. People were just slightly more laissez-faire

in how they addressed race or ethnicity because there was no online community to police it or, more importantly, to provide a platform for brave souls to take a stand, explain how actions negatively affected them, and work for change.

So it was really no surprise at the time to hear this description of Irish culture from a lawyer discussing his Irish-Canadian client on TV. His interview was part of a documentary that aired on the CBC cultural affairs program *Adrienne Clarkson Presents*.

> He was a young guy
> of great spirit who
> had what I perceive
> to be that lyrical Irish
> personality made up
> of various parts. One
> part is he has a creative
> quality, a charm, and
> the other qualities that

are commonplace in that type of personality are things like, perhaps, drinking more than other people do and an enjoyment of fighting.

To sum up, a lawyer called his client a fightin' Irish drinker with the ol' gift o' the gab on a show hosted by Clarkson, who would six years later be appointed governor general of Canada. The documentary also included an interview with the same Irish-Canadian's arresting officer. "I saw him on *Arsenio Hall* and I said to myself, 'Snow? That's not Snow. That's Darrin O'Brien.'"

Yes, the brawling, charming, typical drunken Irish hoodlum was the emerging Canadian dance-hall rap star Darrin "Snow" O'Brien. Clarkson was presenting a documentary on the "twenty-three-year-old white

male from Toronto" and his debut album, *12 Inches of Snow*, a name she delivered with the clued-in hipness of a meteorologist.

And while the casual propagation of tired stereotypes about the Irish might not have piqued the public's ire, they were unsure about Snow. What was the proper reaction to this white rapper? Was he capitalizing on Jamaican culture? Was he racist? Was it racist to judge him on the colour of his skin, even though it was so snow-white that it was reflected in his stage name? Or was his stage name a reference to cocaine? Was this white Canadian rapper a drug addict? Was that why he was in jail? Was that why his video was set in jail? Had he really been in jail or did he just make that up the same way Vanilla Ice tried to get everyone to believe he was stabbed in the butt to increase his street cred? What is Snow singing about in "Informer"? How does he sing so fast? What language is that? Is it racist to ask that? That constant refrain in "Informer"— "A licky boom-boom down" — what does that mean? Is it butt stuff? Because whenever he says that line in the video, they seem to zoom in on shots of booty-shorts-clad dancers seductively rump-shaking.

This is just a sample of the many questions mulled over by a society becoming increasingly aware of the ever-evolving race politics of hip hop culture. Who were we to believe — Adrienne Clarkson, who seemed genuinely bemused by teens' love of this Jamaican wannabe, or Jim Carrey's caustic satire of the video on *In Living Color*? With a parody

Jim Carrey.

entitled "Imposter," Carrey, who was born in Newmarket, Ontario, pulled no punches in harshly critiquing Snow's watered-down reggae by implying he was "One Hit Wonder Bread" and dealing this devastating burn: "Pretending I was a Rasta since I was in jammies / I should paint my face and start belting out 'Mammy.'"

Bryan Adams: white man.

While our sensitivity about race and cultural appropriation was then still maturing, it had come a long way since 1984. No one batted an eyelash that Christmas when Bryan Adams released "Reggae Christmas." If you've been trapped in an attic for the past thirty-five years and are unfamiliar with one of the world's bestselling music artists of all time, picture a white man. Wrong. Picture him even whiter. Adams, who was born to British parents in Kingston, Ontario, in 1959, has the kind of lily-pale complexion that Coppertone has built an empire trying to protect.

"Reggae Christmas" was the B-side to Adams's popular "Merry Christmas" single. The video is memorable because it stars Pee-wee Herman wearing a dreadlocks wig under a Santa hat and dancing with MTV VJs and dozens of others as Adams performs the song live. The crowd is overwhelmingly white, although if you look closely you can spot two or three black people in the video. You could push the number up to four if you included the Mr. T doll Herman gifts to VJ Alan Hunter. ("I pity the poor fool who don't get Pee-wee no presents," Herman intones.)

Adams may have received a pass because this was a B-side, practically a novelty song. Yet the song's "hey mon" refrain and wishes of "a merry Christmas and a reggae New Year to you," should have set off alarm bells, if not for crossing questionable cultural thresholds, then certainly for being off-the-charts cheesy.

In Snow's defence, "Informer" wasn't a crass commercial ploy to rip off another culture for personal gain. Born in Toronto and raised in its notorious Allenbury Gardens public housing project, he was bewitched as a young teen by his neighbours' Jamaican dance-hall tapes and spent hours learning to imitate the patois-heavy singing style.

He loved it, studied it, honoured it. He wasn't imitating it; he was inhabiting it. He deejayed local parties, where he befriended Jamaican-born DJ Marvin Prince. The pair caught the attention of MC Shan, who'd had a hit in '85 with "Feed the World" (not to be confused with that year's international super-hit "We Are the World" by USA for Africa). MC Shan's support was a factor that lead to Snow's record contract with Motorjam/Elektra and his debut album.

But unlike Vanilla Ice, whose team fabricated a police record to up his street cred, Snow was actually in prison when his single was released. He was facing a charge of attempted murder that was eventually dropped. Turns out "a licky boom-boom down" means "I'm gonna beat that stool pigeon," according to Snow's ghetto-precocious preteen brother in the *Adrienne Clarkson* documentary. Turns out a "stool pigeon" is a snitch. The whole song tells the tale of Snow's false imprisonment — and he ups his authenticity by stating he's from Toronto, not Jamaica, in the lyrics, although his delivery is so fast you could be excused for missing it.

"Informer" spent seven consecutive weeks in the number one spot on the *Billboard* Hot 100. Snow was never able to replicate its massive international success, but that was not unusual for practitioners of the genre at the time. Dozens of rap and hip hop artists emerged in that era and then dropped off the map, including Vanilla Ice, Kriss Kross, MC Hammer, Canibus, The Pharcyde, Black Sheep, and House of Pain, a white American hip hop group featuring the Irish-American member Danny Boy.

Hip hop culture and attitudes about who's allowed to sing what have developed since the early '90s and are constantly evolving. Ottawa trio A Tribe Called Red experienced explosive popularity starting in the early '10s with their modern mix of hip hop, reggae, and traditional First Nations chanting and drumming. In spite of their success in connecting listeners to this extraordinary cultural gem, they too have faced criticism about cultural exploitation. Traditionalist First Nations people have questioned their recontextualized use of sacred honour songs and denounced their performance at venues that serve alcohol, which is a no-go at powwows. Other friction has come from non–First Nations fans attending A Tribe Called Red shows in dollar-store headdresses and war paint. The group put the kibosh on the

A Tribe Called Red.

practice, which they view as a caricature of their culture. It's something they say happens way too much already in Hollywood depictions of Aboriginal people, like Johnny Depp's portrayal of "Indian" sidekick Tonto in 2013's *The Lone Ranger*, as well as in sports team names and logos. A Tribe Called Red member Ian "DJ NDN" Campeau filed a complaint with the Human Rights Tribunal of Ontario in 2013 that led to a name change for the Ottawa-area Nepean Redskins Football Club.

Still, A Tribe Called Red sees each performance as a chance to build relationships and understanding among their diverse fandom. "There's still a ways to go," Campeau told *The Walrus* in 2013. "But conversations are happening, and that's the most important thing, because they weren't happening before."

As well as being an author, broadcaster, former governor general, and total boss with a veritable alphabet after her name, The Right Honourable Adrienne Clarkson, PC CC CMM COM CD FRSC (hon) FRAIC (hon) FRCPSC (hon), is the child of Hong Kong immigrants who lost everything in the Second World War. "Individuals are not independent of each other. We have individual rights, but we also have duties to others," she said in "Belonging: The Paradox of Citizenship," the 2014 CBC

Massey Lecture. "We are most fully human, most truly ourselves, most authentically individual, when we commit to the community. It is in the mirror of our community — the street, the neighbourhood, the town, the country — that we find our best selves." And if we can find ourselves there through music, then so much the better.

And if you can find yourself there through a quiz, well then, this next section is very conveniently located for you:

. . . .

1. **Who was the first Canadian rapper to be signed to a major American label?**

     a) Michie Mee
     b) Le Boyfriend
     c) Snow
     d) Kardinal Offishall

. . . .

2. **How many centimetres are in twelve inches of snow?**

     a) 12
     b) 18.24
     c) 30.48
     d) 40

. . . .

3. **Which Canadian musicians have appeared on *Trailer Park Boys*?**

     a) Sebastian Bach, formerly of Skid Row, and Rita MacNeil
     b) Alex Lifeson of Rush and Brian Vollmer from Helix
     c) Snow and DJ Marvin Prince
     d) both a) and b)

. . . .

4. **Which TV star had Snow record a version of his/her show's theme song?**

     a) Alan Thicke
     b) Drew Carey
     c) Roseanne Barr
     d) Michael J. Fox

ANSWERS

1. Who was the first Canadian rapper to be signed to a major American label?

Answer: a) Michie Mee

Canada's first woman of hip hop, the Jamaican-born, Toronto-raised Michie Mee, blazed the trail when she signed with First Priority/Atlantic Records in 1988. Quebec's Le Boyfriend released *Rapper Chic (je rap en français)* in 1990 on Canadian label Station 12/ Musicor. Snow released *12 Inches of Snow* on the American label Motorjam/Elektra in 1993. Canada's long-time hip hop ambassador, Kardinal Offishal, signed with MCA Records in the States in 2000.

2. How many centimetres are in twelve inches of snow?

Answer: c) 30.48

Your twelve-inch ruler is about thirty centimetres long. Give yourself a bonus point if you learned that on TVO's 1978 program *Report Metric*, starring Heather Conkie.

3. Which Canadian musicians have appeared on *Trailer Park Boys*?

Answer: d) both a) and b)

Peterborough-born Sebastian Bach appeared in season 7 as a prospective weed buyer. Rita MacNeil of Sydney, Nova Scotia, played herself in a 2004 episode of *Trailer Park Boys*, in which she's held at gunpoint and forced to harvest weed. In 2003, Alex Lifeson played himself in an episode that sees him kidnapped after Bubbles is cheated out of getting Rush tickets. He also played an undercover cop in a 2009 show. Snow and DJ Marvin Prince have never appeared on *Trailer Park Boys,* but after watching the *Adrienne Clarkson Presents* documentary, which visits Snow in his Toronto housing project and features an interview with his mom, it's clear that Snow would be a natural fit. You could be excused for mistaking scenes in *Trailer Park Boys* featuring the J-Roc character, a white rapper who lives with his mother, as a shot-for-shot recreation of the *Adrienne Clarkson* documentary.

• • • • • • • • • • • • • • •

4. Which TV star had Snow record a version of his/her show's theme song?

ANSWER: b) Drew Carey

Snow recorded a version of *The Drew Carey Show's* theme song, "Moon Over Parma," which opened the sitcom in 2002. A spokesman for Virgin Records said a demo of the theme was played for a *Drew Carey Show* staff member, "and within minutes the entire cast and crew including Drew was grooving to the song."

Truly, anything is possible.

12

"WHEELCHAIR JIMMY": STARTED FROM DEGRASSI, NOW HE'S DRIZZY

Soap Opera Rapid Aging Syndrome is a trope used so often by daytime drama writers that it's just referred to by the acronym SORAS now, because people in the rapid-aging business try to save time however they can.

You may have noticed SORAS on one of your favourite afternoon stories or even on a prime-time show. SORAS explains how *The Young and the Restless*'s Billy Abbott was born in 1993 but was seventeen by the end of the millennium. It's the reason why *As the World*

Turns's Tom Hughes was born in 1961 but by 1970 he was a college grad and a Nam vet. It's a ridiculous, amateur loophole of a writing device that screenwriters employ out of sheer desperation to avoid writing for or working with children in general, and tweens specifically. Babies are cute. Preschoolers are precocious. Preteens are runty and awkward with pre-braces teeth and terrible hair. No one wants to see their drama.

When *The Kids of Degrassi Street* debuted in 1979, it was like a secret portal into the lives of SORAS casualties. This is what children look like on TV. Real children playing characters their own age, acting out dramas relevant to them. It was terrible.

It's liberating to say *The Kids of Degrassi Street* was terrible. You should try it. Criticizing the series is taboo because it's the foundation of a culturally important franchise, it showed an authentic depiction of children's lives, it was well-received by those outside our borders, and, well, it stars *children,* for heaven's sake. This was adventurous in 1979.

Also adventurous in 1979? Grooving to the fresh beat of The Sugarhill Gang's "Rapper's Delight." Released on September 16, 1979, it became the first rap single to enter the *Billboard* Top 40, and it introduced hip hop to audiences around the world.

Now let's SORAS our way to 1986, the year Aubrey Drake Graham was born to Toronto teacher Sandi Graham and her husband, Memphis musician Dennis Graham. It was the same year that gangsta rap emerged as the dominant force in hip hop. Ice-T released the single "6 in the Mornin'," a bouncy ballad about police, players, pistols, pimps, and, of course, stabbing your fellow cell dweller right in the eye. The influential track helped to ignite the gangsta rap phenomenon, a harder-edged, more aggressive style of hip hop that glorified thug life. Meanwhile, the kids of Degrassi were positively writhing in their awkward televised puberty as they prepared to enter the ever-earnest *Degrassi Junior High*, the next instalment in the television series, which debuted in 1987.

Let's rapidly age now right through to 2001, when *Degrassi: The Next Generation* rebooted on CTV, featuring the now-fifteen-year-old Drake playing the character of affable, affluent high school basketball star Jimmy Brooks. Drake made his debut on the show wearing an oversized white hoodie and dribbling a basketball that a classmate swipes from him mid-bounce. Drake's character carries on as

though it didn't happen, miming making a basket on the schoolyard trash can before sidling up to reassure a new kid at school by telling him everything's going to be okay. Then he playfully punches the kid's shoulder and says "A'iite?" In response, the new kid wordlessly gets up with the express purpose of moving away from him. Drake really started from the bottom.

Meanwhile, the era's biggest hip hop stars were now street-cred-heavy gangsta rappers with backstories comprised largely of deeds cut-and-pasted from their lengthy criminal records. It was gangsta rap and it was written by gangsters. There was no room for phonies. Rapper 50 Cent started selling crack at age twelve and has been shot nine times. L.A. gangbanger and *Billboard* hit-maker the Game has been shot five times. Rappers

Biggie Smalls and Tupac Shakur, members of warring hip hop factions, were both shot to death in murder cases that have never been solved.

Hip hop stars of the previous era had no chance. The order of the day was nihilistic ghetto gang gunplay, frustrated social protest, enthusiastic misogyny, and crack. When Vanilla Ice's puffed-up rap sheet turned out to be fabricated, the lie virtually ended his career, because even more than street cred, hip hop values authenticity. When MC Hammer tried to go ghetto hard to attract the new gangsta rap audience, listeners could smell his inauthenticity from miles away. Hammer had, after all, starred in his own Saturday morning children's cartoon, *Hammerman*, about a youth centre worker who owns a pair of anthropomorphized magical dancing shoes that transform him into the superhero Hammerman. It's hard to establish yourself retroactively as a badass after that.

As a passionate hip hop fan and aspiring rapper, Drake must have realized it would be equally difficult to establish himself as a badass after starring in a Canadian teen soap opera, even though his character got shot in season three. Not only was Drake starring on a Canadian teen soap opera, but because of his relatively comfortable, gunshot-free Toronto upbringing, his *Degrassi* character now had more street cred than he did.

Off set, Drake idolized rap king Jay Z, who had grown up in one of New York City's most dangerous housing projects, where he sold crack as a child. At age twelve, Jay Z shot his own brother in the shoulder for stealing his jewellery. The rapper himself had been shot at three times, but his assailants had missed. His debut

That serious Rosie O'Donnell street cred: Drake stands next to the talk show host during a *Degrassi* event in 2007.

album, *Reasonable Doubt*, was released in 1996, and by 2002, at age thirty-three, the Grammy winner owned his own record label, clothing line, and movie production company that together generated almost half a billion dollars a year in sales.

Back in Toronto, Drake was further than ever from establishing street cred or embarking on a serious rap career. By 2004, his *Degrassi* character was known as "Wheelchair Jimmy," a lazy nickname that demeans the character and wheelchair users in general by defining them solely by their use of a wheelchair. Plus it's the least hard core of any nickname that could be bestowed

Jay Z in 2001.

Wheelchair Jimmy, who formerly played on the Degrassi school basketball team, now starred in storylines about his burgeoning music career. In a case of *Degrassi* imitating life imitating *Degrassi*, both Drake and his TV alter ego were embarking on careers in hip hop in 2006.

Drake had none of the street cred that had been a prerequisite for hip hop success for the previous decade-and-a-half. Having had his adolescence broadcast on TV, plus the evolution of the internet, made his resume and bio easily accessible public knowledge. But like a desperate soap opera writer ready to invoke SORAS, Graham had found a loophole to excuse his adolescent experience: even beyond street cred, hip hop values authenticity. So he doubled down on that.

Drake independently released his first mixtape, *Room*

on a gunshot victim who seeks to legitimize his struggle. Anything would have been cooler: WC Jimmy Jam, J Throne Cobra, Quint Jimmy Roller a.k.a. Krazy Kart Styles, anything.

for Improvement, as a free online download. The title is the antithesis of gangsta rap braggadocio. The distribution method was the opposite of the commercialized, "dollar dollar bill, y'all" refrain of hard-hustlin' rappers. The lyrics showed a more emotive, vulnerable MC who was ready to get real on a whole other level.

This kind of risky innovation was welcome in the industry. At the time, music sales across all genres were declining because of the advent of digital music file sharing, but rap sales were falling the hardest, and even established acts were posting low returns. Between 2000 and 2007, rap sales had dropped a whopping 44 percent. Industry leaders floundered in their search for solutions as the realization dawned that the demand for gangsta rap had cooled and audiences wanted something new.

Drake in 2006.

Whether he knew it or not, Drake had done that thing corporate CEOs are always saying Wayne Gretzky said: "Skate to where the puck is going, not where it has been." By looking beyond street cred and embracing authenticity more than anyone before, he had turned the hip hop ethos back on itself.

Comeback Season, Drake's second mixtape, was released online in 2007. Drake was attracting an increasing amount of attention. Every time the press and public goaded the rapper for being from Toronto, for being from Canada, for appearing on a teen soap opera, for being a mamma's boy, every time he was criticized for never selling crack or getting shot, he didn't only admit it, he didn't try to explain it, he didn't even apologize for

Drake embracing his inner nerd at the 2014 ESPYs.

Drake and his fly bowtie on stage at the 2011 JUNO Awards.

it; he just owned it. He owned it *hard*.

He repped Toronto wherever he went. The Toronto Blue Jays saw sales of their caps soar stateside after Drake wore one on the cover of *Vibe* magazine in 2009. He hosted the adorably cheesy JUNO Awards in 2011 and walked the red carpet with his mom. In 2013, he became the Toronto Raptors' global ambassador.

In response to being called a mama's boy, he doubled down on how real he could be. He put his mom in his videos and liberally peppered his Instagram feed with

Drake with Zach LaVine of the Minnesota Timberwolves and Raptors' mascot The Raptor at the 2016 NBA All-Star Weekend Slam Dunk Contest.

pics of them together. On *The Tonight Show*, he called his mom a top-shelf lady and bragged about her Scrabble prowess. He was dazzlingly, unbelievably authentic. He was fearless in the face of his own dorkdom. Compared to the macho gangsta rap stars he had idolized, he was Superman in Bizarro World; he was George Costanza doing the opposite; he had sailed so far east he had arrived west.

And he *had* arrived. His second mixtape caught the attention of four-time Grammy-winning hip hop superstar Lil Wayne. A major-label bidding war ensued. Drake's first studio album, 2010's *Thank Me Later*, debuted at number one on the *Billboard* 200 and featured a collaboration with his idol, Jay Z. It was the start of a record-breaking career that has made Drake one of the most successful rappers in history.

Drake surrounded by adoring fans at the 2013 MTV Video Music Awards.

#YOLO! Go zero to a hundred real quick with your woes because when I hear that hotline bling, that can only mean it's quiz time:

- - - - - - - - - - - - - - - -

1. **True or false: Historica Canada, the organization that produces the *Heritage Minutes* PSAs illustrating important moments in Canadian history, created a mash-up of Minutes to honour Drake.**

- - - - - - - - - - - - - - - -

2. **As the Toronto Raptors' global ambassador, Drake opened an exclusive sports club at the Air Canada Centre. After whom did he name it?**
   - a) his mom
   - b) Wheelchair Jimmy
   - c) Jay Z
   - d) his grandparents

- - - - - - - - - - - - - - - -

3. **Which fellow Canadian former child star was the executive producer of Drake's mixtape "So Far Gone"?**
   - a) Michael Cera
   - b) Alanis Morissette
   - c) Ryan Gosling
   - d) Noah Shebib

- - - - - - - - - - - - - - - -

4. **How many albums has Drake sold?**
   - a) one million
   - b) two million
   - c) more than three million
   - d) more than five million

ANSWERS

1. True or false: Historica Canada, the organization that produces the *Heritage Minutes* PSAs illustrating important moments in Canadian history, created a mash-up of Minutes to honour Drake.

Answer: true

The organization created "the most Canadian mash-up of all time" in March 2015. The video reassembles samples of video and dialogue from fifty-three original *Heritage Minutes* so that the dialogue mimics the lyrics of Drake's 2013 hit song "Started from the Bottom."

2. As the Toronto Raptors' global ambassador, Drake opened an exclusive sports club at the Air Canada Centre. After whom did he name it?

Answer: d) his grandparents

Drake unveiled the Sher Club on Instagram with the following message: "Rest in peace to my grandparents Rueben and Evelyn Sher."

3. Which fellow Canadian former child star was the executive producer of Drake's mixtape "So Far Gone"?

Answer: d) Noah Shebib

Noah "40" Shebib reportedly earned his nickname for his "40 days and 40 nights"–worthy work ethic, not his love of 40-ouncers of malt liquor. This deviation from the standard hip hop narrative puts him in good stead with Drake. Shebib appeared on *Wind at My Back* and *Goosebumps,* among other Canadian TV fare, before switching his focus to music. He's since produced work with Beyoncé, Lil Wayne, Alicia Keys, and Jamie Foxx, and is the co-founder with Drake of the OVO Sound record label.

Michael Cera of Brampton, Ontario, first appeared in a Tim Hortons summer camp TV commercial before going on to star in the TV series *Arrested Development* and movies like *Superbad, Juno,* and *Scott Pilgrim vs. the World.* Alanis Morissette of Ottawa appeared on *You Can't Do That on Television* before becoming the "Canadian Debbie Gibson" and then evolving into the quintessential chart-topping alt-rock queen. Hollywood heartthrob Ryan

Gosling was born in London, Ontario and lived in Cornwall and Burlington before acing an audition in Montreal for the *Mickey Mouse Club*. He starred on the series alongside Justin Timberlake, Britney Spears, and Christina Aguilera before rising to fame in 2004 after starring opposite fellow Londoner Rachel McAdams in the now-classic romance movie *The Notebook*. Now both McAdams and Drake make the 6ix their home.

• • • • • • • • • • • • • • •

4. How many albums has Drake sold?

Answer: d) more than five million

Drake has sold more than five million albums worldwide. His 2016 album, *Views,* has sold more than a million copies alone.

ROUND FOUR
Weirdos

THESE WERE ACTUALLY
CANADIAN PRIME MINISTERS?

13

SIR JOHN A. MACDONALD: FOUNDER OF THE "GO HOME, DAD, YOU'RE DRUNK" MEME

One thing that we can all agree on is that Sir John Alexander Macdonald was the first prime minister of Canada and he was in charge from 1867 to 1873 and again from 1878 until 1891. That's nineteen years at the helm; only William Lyon Mackenzie King served longer. His champions will tell you he built a national government and a cross-country railroad. His detractors will remind you he was a drunk who accepted bribes and ordered the execution of Metis leader Louis Riel.

But it's generally agreed that he was the father of Canadian Confederation. So, for better or for worse, Macdonald is Canada's dad. Prior to taking up politics, he practised law, so in an homage to his vocation, let's examine the extent of his total "dadness" through the presentation of this evidence:

EXHIBIT A: CHILDREN

Okay, Macdonald married and had kids with his first cousin, Isabella Clark. Get over it. It was de rigueur at the time. They married in 1843, and in 1847 they welcomed their first child, John Jr., who died in infancy. In 1850, they had another son, Hugh. Seven years later, his wife passed after a lengthy illness. Macdonald remarried in 1867, this time to his secretary's sister, Agnes Bernard, who gave birth to their

Sir John A. Macdonald's daughter, Mary.

daughter, Mary, in 1869. She was born with developmental issues and was never able to walk, but by all accounts, Macdonald absolutely doted on her.

Exhibit B: Dad Jokes

You're likely familiar with the brand of corny jokes that only dads tell. For the uninitiated, observe here the quintessential dad joke: The kid says, "I'm hungry." The dad replies, "Hi Hungry, I'm Dad." It is this level of cheesy wordplay that Macdonald employed with abandon, as witnessed by these examples:

- A women's suffrage activist asked Macdonald why men could vote but women couldn't. He paused, then replied quizzically, "Madame, I cannot conceive."
- While attending a senator's funeral, an aspiring senator approached Macdonald to say he'd like to take the man's place. Macdonald told him it was too late; the coffin was already nailed shut.
- In conversation about the wealth of railway magnate/political enemy Sir Hugh Allan, it was mentioned that Allan might as well spend all his money since he couldn't take it with him. Macdonald said it would melt if he did.

There are those who argue that Macdonald is by far our wittiest prime minister, but it is clear that those who advance this argument are themselves dads.

Exhibit C: Dad Jeans

High-waisted, functional denim pants, with or without pleats or a belt-based phone holster, are wardrobe staples of dads everywhere. Of course, jeans did not start to gain widespread popularity until John Diefenbaker moved into the prime minister's office in 1957. But photographs do show Macdonald in hella high-waisted slacks, and the timepiece he tucks into his vest indicates that, were he a modern dad, he might wear his phone externally, or even (gasp!) *employ a fanny pack*.

Exhibit D: Dad Bod

Not morbidly obese but no longer in peak physical condition, the squishy dad bod is soft in the middle. It is the body of a family man whose metabolism has slowed down; he's replaced football practice with fantasy

Exhibit C.

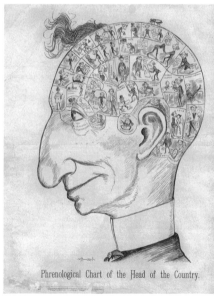

Phrenological Chart of the Head of the Country.

This dad's got a lot on his mind.

170

football, and yet he still downs drinks and puts away pizza like a teen. Macdonald was an average physical specimen who almost certainly never engaged in fantasy football and probably never got to eat pizza, but he did drink. Yes. Yes he did.

Exhibit E: Go Home, Dad, You're Drunk

We've all heard the joke about the drunk guy who stumbles into a bar and razzes a patron by saying, "I had sex with your mother!" To which the patron replies, "Go home, Dad, you're drunk." This colloquial punchline has spun into a popular internet meme in the "fail/you're doing it wrong" genre.

Likely there were many occasions on which Hugh and Mary would have liked to tell

their esteemed patriarch, "Go home, Dad, you're drunk." Here is a small sampling of such occasions:

- Dad is totally legless at an official luncheon for Prince Arthur in 1868. Let's say it together: Go home, Dad, you're drunk.
- Dad is so hammered during a political debate that he throws up on stage then blames his opponent's policies for making him sick. Go home, Dad, you're drunk!
- Dad threatens to beat up an opponent in the House of Commons with this weak-arsed threat: "I'll lick him faster than hell can scorch a feather!" All together now: Go home, Dad, you're DRUNK!
- The Fenians tried to gain Irish independence by invading the Niagara Peninsula in 1866 in

a convoluted attempt to trade it back to Britain in exchange for Ireland. Macdonald, then Upper Canada's minister of militia, was too drunk to read the piles of urgent, panicky telegrams. Luckily the invasion failed. Let's drink to that! But not you, Dad. You've already had enough. Head home now, okay?

- Dad gets severe acute pancreatitis almost certainly due to his crazy-high alcohol intake. Seriously, Dad? We love you. C'mon. Get help. At home. Go there now. You're drunk.

Luckily, Macdonald's second wife undertook the momentous challenge of weaning him off the bottle. She gradually succeeded, and he spent the last decade or so of his life pretty solidly sober.

Researchers now theorize that multiple sclerosis might have been the long illness that claimed Macdonald's first wife. Her untimely death is one of the many family tragedies that Macdonald endured and to which biographers often attribute his alcoholism.

But had his first wife/first cousin survived until Canada's Confederation in 1867, then she would have been Canada's mom, and then Canada's uncle would also have been its grandfather, and the nation would only have had one set of great-grandparents. This is solid conversation fodder next time you're sipping a cold one with your dad, and while you're at it, why not give him this quiz? Yes, he can turn it into a drinking game if he wants. Just make sure he gets home safe.

• • • • • • • • • • • • • • •

1. **Which historical figures married their cousins?**

    a) Charles Darwin, Rudy Giuliani, and Edgar Allan Poe

    b) Franklin Delano Roosevelt, Saddam Hussein, and Thomas Jefferson

    c) Albert Einstein, Queen Elizabeth II, and Abraham Maslow

    d) all of the above

• • • • • • • • • • • • • • •

2. **True or false: As of 2015, about 75 percent of Canadians drink at least occasionally.**

3. **Macdonald's doctor, John Robinson Dickson, was an abstainer who worked to cut off the flow of alcohol at**

    a) Kingston Penitentiary

    b) Queen's University

    c) Kingston's Rockwood Asylum

    d) all of the above

• • • • • • • • • • • • • • •

4. **Which Canadian prime minister had nine children?**

    a) John Abbott

    b) John Sparrow David Thompson

    c) Mackenzie Bowell

    d) both b) and c)

ROUND FOUR – WEIRDOS

ANSWERS

. . . .

1. Which historical figures married their cousins?

Answer: d) all of the above

Seriously, all of these people married a cousin. Evolution scientist Charles Darwin married his first cousin, Emma Wedgwood. Former New York City mayor Rudy Giuliani married his second cousin once removed, Regina Peruggi. Writer Edgar Allan Poe married his first cousin, Virginia Clemm. American president Franklin D. Roosevelt married his fifth cousin once removed, Eleanor Roosevelt. (Sure, "fifth cousin once removed"

Albert and Elsa: kissing cousins.

makes it sound like a pretty distant relative, but consider this: her last name was Roosevelt *before* they were married.) Iraqi president Saddam Hussein married his first cousin, Sajida Talfah. American Founding Father Thomas Jefferson married his third cousin, Martha Wayles. Albert Einstein married his first cousin on his mother's side who was also his second cousin on his father's side, Elsa Löwenthal. (Löwenthal was Elsa's first husband's last name. She was born with the last name Einstein. Biographers have referred to them euphemistically as "a close-knit family.")

Queen Elizabeth II married her second cousin once removed, Prince Philip, Duke of Edinburgh. Famed psychologist Abraham Maslow married his first cousin, Bertha Goodman.

• • • • • • • • • • • • • •

2. True or false: As of 2015, about 75 percent of Canadians drink at least occasionally.

Answer: true

Three-quarters of us drink at least once in a while. Our reputation as a beer-loving country is supported by the stat that beer and ale account for 51 percent of the alcohol we drink. We don't drink nearly as much wine as some of our European pals: Canadians drink an average of nine litres of wine each year, compared with sixty-two litres in Portugal and sixty-seven litres in France.

. . . .
3. Macdonald's doctor, John
   Robinson Dickson, was an
   abstainer who worked to cut
   off the flow of alcohol at

**Answer: c) Kingston's
Rockwood Asylum**

Among his many accomplishments, Dickson turned off the taps at the Rockwood Criminal Lunatic Asylum in Kingston. The institution housed convicts who'd gone insane at the penitentiary, mentally unsound local folk, lepers, and promiscuous women. All wore the standard-issue canvas uniforms that boldly bore the label LUNATIC. Staff worked not to punish patients, nor to rehabilitate them, but to calm them. Common treatments included restraints, blistering, leeching, enemas, lobotomies, and bloodletting. The institution's

only M.D., Dr. Litchfield, employed a standard daily routine that involved "a pretty free use of alcohol by day and sedative by night." Today, the building houses Providence Manor, a long-term care home for seniors.

You lose a point if you guessed b) Queen's University. Just the thought of that institution running dry is hard to hold in your mind even for a moment.

. . . .
4. Which Canadian prime
   minister had nine children?

Answer: d) both b) and c)

Canada's third prime minister, John Abbott, was in office for almost a year and a half, between 1891 and 1892. He and his wife Mary Bethune (yes, she is related to Dr. Norman Bethune) had only eight children: Frances,

John, William, Henry, Charles, Alice, Arthur, and Harriet.

John Sparrow David Thompson took over from Abbott in 1892 and served until his sudden death in office in 1894. His wife, Annie Affleck, was mother to John, Joseph, Mary Aloysia, Mary Helena, Annie, Frances, David, and two children who died in infancy. After her husband's passing, she co-founded the National Council of Women and served as president. She also served as governor of the Victorian Order of Nurses.

When Thompson died, Mackenzie Bowell was the most senior cabinet minister, so the governor general appointed him to take over. He became our fifth prime minister and served until 1896. He and his wife, Harriet Moore, also had nine kids: Charles, Evalyn, John, Alice, George, Louisa, Caroline, Elizabeth, and Anna. And after all this, if you're still looking for baby name ideas, Canada is nice for a boy or a girl.

14

WILLIAM LYON MACKENZIE KING: INSPIRED SPIRITUALIST, BIG, BIG FAN OF DOGS

Canada's House of Commons is hallowed ground within our esteemed Parliament Buildings in Ottawa. It's where our elected members of Parliament convene to undertake the solemn work of governing. Bills are debated, votes are undertaken, constituents' views are represented, and national issues are discussed.

For example, on Friday, March 4, 1977, Howard Johnston, MP for Okanagan–Kootenay, put the following motion to the House of Commons:

Mr. Speaker, I rise under the provisions of Standing Order 43 to raise a matter of urgent and pressing necessity arising out of an attempt by the CBC to conjure up the spirit of the departed Right Honourable William Lyon Mackenzie King, not knowing whether that exercise was attempted at the request of the prime minister, Mr. Trudeau, or whether it was an attempt by that Crown corporation to bring itself once again into the good graces of the Liberal Party. In either event I move, seconded by the hon. member for Provencher, Mr. Epp: That this House urge the CBC to cease and desist from further such attempts, believing that this country is in sufficient danger from the ghastly mismanagement of the present administration without compounding the problem by obtaining the ghostly advice of the prime minister's unlamented predecessor.[1]

No, this motion was not met with riotous laughter. No, the Honourable Howard Johnston was not having a stroke. No, that's not a gag name, that's his real name, and anyway the hotel chain is Howard Johnson (without the "t"). Yes, he probably got called HoJo all the time anyway. And even with those questions addressed, there are so many more:

1. Did the CBC really try to conjure up the spirit of the

---

1. Howard Earl Johnston, Progressive Conservative, March 4, 1977, Routine Proceedings, CBC: http://j.mp/2b1GxO4.

departed Right Honourable William Lyon Mackenzie King?

Yes. In the spring of 1977, CBC Radio's *Sunday Morning* program conducted a séance at Laurier House in an attempt to conjure the spirit of former Liberal prime minister, the late Mackenzie King.

2. What's Laurier House?

It's — wait, what? That's the least interesting part of this. Why are you asking about that? Didn't you see that part about "conducting a séance?"

3. Okay, why did the CBC conduct a séance?

Mackenzie King was really into spiritualism, but he kept it secret from the public. He conducted séances almost every night for years. He also kept a weirdly detailed (but very dryly written) diary. He wrote in it almost every day. For fifty-seven years. And in his diary, he said that he'd like to communicate with the living after he'd died. So CBC answered the call.

4. And … just remind me, who is Mackenzie King again?

He's our longest-serving prime minister. He spent twenty-two years in office and was at the helm during the Second World War. He's on the fifty-dollar bill. He's kind of a big deal.

5. And he's a kook?

No, actually; spiritualism was very common pastime for polite society in the first part of the twentieth century. It was partly a way of coping with profound grief at the human cost of the

First World War. Canada lost about 60,000 citizens during the conflict, which raged from 1914 to 1918. Over in the U.K., Sherlock Holmes creator Sir Arthur Conan Doyle, who lost a son in the war, was big into spiritualism, and corresponded with mystic/dentist Samuel Aykroyd. There are reports that Lincoln held séances at the White House. It was a thing.

Mackenzie King's diaries reveal that he regularly conducted séances to contact his mother and his, um, dogs.

6. So he's a kook.

It sounds kooky, but consider this: In a 2013 experiment conducted by the *Guardian* newspaper in Britain, a house cat named Orlando outperformed a team of stock-picking professionals in an investment management competition. Paul the Octopus predicted the winners of every match in the 2010 World Cup. Heidi, a cross-eyed opossum, predicted the winners of three Academy Awards categories in 2011. If Canada's destiny in the most widespread war in history was guided by discussions with a beloved late Irish terrier named Pat (or Pat's successors, Pat II and Pat III), who are we to criticize?

7. Getting back to HoJo's complaint: did Prime Minister Trudeau ask the CBC to Ouija up Mackenzie King?

All signs point to no. CBC Radio launched the *Sunday Morning* program in 1976 with the promise of delivering a dazzling array of hard news, drama, documentary, arts reviews, and concerts, the likes of which radio airwaves had never seen. Program director Margaret Lyons vowed that *Sunday Morning* would be the newspaper of the air. Producer Mark Starowicz proclaimed, "The cassette tape recorder is the Instamatic of radio." Lofty selling points all.

Each episode of *Sunday Morning* featured a drama from their News Theatre, and the first two to air were part of a series

Irish terrier Pat with his person, William Lyon Mackenzie King. So beloved was the pup that he even appeared in a wartime tourism ad alongside Mackenzie King.

re-enacting some of Mackenzie King's many diary entries about séances. The diaries of Mackenzie King, who passed away in 1950, had been gradually released to the public throughout the 1970s. *Sunday Morning* sought to capitalize on Canadians' fascination with King's secret personal life, and particularly his devotion to spiritualism. The séance to contact Mackenzie King was an outgrowth of the News Theatre dramatizations, and there's no evidence that Trudeau was a driving force. As a Crown corporation, the CBC operates at arm's length from the government.

8. Is *Sunday Morning* a comedy show?

No. The twelve-minute broadcast of *Sunday Morning*'s attempt to contact Mackenzie King demonstrates that this séance was undertaken in solemn earnestness and with respect for the medium, Geraldine Smith. Smith was twenty-six at the time and a noted psychic in Brampton, Ontario, where she undertook readings on people as well as horses. She was also a psychic consultant for the police force.

9. This sounds like a real *Scooby-Doo* kind of thing. Was there, like, a crystal ball there?

Yes. Smith also held two dog collars as she entered her trance-like state.

10. Was the séance successful in contacting Mackenzie King?

After spending the day "generating her own energy for the evening," Smith spent a further fifteen minutes of heavy breathing "getting into the alpha level of her brain so that Mackenzie King can come through."

First, she made contact with Mackenzie King's grandmother, Christine; his dog, Little Pat; and his brother, Max. Then she made contact with Mackenzie King himself, and CBC Radio producer Angus McLellan was permitted to ask the spirit questions.

He began by asking, "Have you been aware of the Canadian scene since you left?" The spirit of Mackenzie King via Smith replied in a low voice: "My most cherished wish, the one thing that I strove for, that was one of the most important things to me in my life, was that the French and the Canadians be together. And I find myself seeing much unhappiness." McLellan then asked, "Would you have any advice for Mr. Trudeau about Quebec?" and Mackenzie King's alleged spirit responded, "If it were me in office at this time, I would highly recommend that he speak with peaceful words, then go to all of the officials. I do not see separation; however, there will be many battles before that is decided."

Perhaps Mackenzie King was foreseeing the Quebec sovereignty referendums of 1980 and 1995, but before McLellan could ask for details, Mackenzie King complained of hostile vibrations and asked for the room to be cleared. In the ensuing process of clearing the room of media and spectators, during which a reporter tried to hide behind a couch, contact with Mackenzie King's spirit was lost, and the experiment drew to a close.

11. So they made contact with Mackenzie King and all they talked about was Quebec

separatism? Seems like MP HoJo should have risen in chambers to complain they didn't address winning lottery numbers or the Stanley Cup Playoffs. Still, that part where he calls Mackenzie King "un-lamented" is pretty harsh.

The Canadian House of Commons has bad manners. In 1971, Prime Minister Pierre Trudeau dropped the f-bomb ("Fuddleduddle," he maintained). In 1985, Tory cabinet minister John Crosbie told Liberal MP Sheila Copps to "just quiet down, baby." Copps demanded he withdraw his remarks, stating, "I'm not his baby, and I'm nobody's baby." In 2011, then Member of Parliament Justin Trudeau called Conservative Environment Minister Peter Kent a "piece of shit." Still, to say our longest-running prime minister was unmourned and his passing not regretted seemed particularly mean-spirited.

12. Did the motion pass?

After MP Johnson raised the motion, the Speaker of the House, Liberal James Alexander Jerome, called for order and asked if there was unanimous consent for the motion. The honourable members did not grant unanimous consent, and the House went on to discuss the matters of abortion accessibility, mercury pollution, and the United States' Securities Exchange Commission's investigation into Boeing.

13. This chapter has already been full of questions. Is there going to be a quiz, too?

The universe is full of questions — just like this quiz:

1. But seriously, what is Laurier House?

    a) the prime minister's official residence

    b) the leader of the Opposition's official residence

    c) the governor general's official residence

    d) a probably haunted old yellow-brick place in Ottawa's Sandy Hill 'hood

2. Whom did the grandson of Sir Arthur Conan Doyle's mystic pen pal play in *Ghostbusters*?

    a) Peter Venkman

    b) Raymond "Ray" Stantz

    c) Egon Spengler

    d) Winston Zeddemore

3. How many university degrees did Mackenzie King earn?

    a) zero

    b) two

    c) three

    d) five

4. I was really hoping this chapter would have a connection to Lorne Greene. Does it?

    a) yes

    b) no

ANSWERS

• • • • • • • • • • • • • • • •

1. But seriously, what is Laurier House?

Answer: d) a probably haunted old yellow-brick place in Ottawa's Sandy Hill 'hood

It's a yellow-brick Victorian mansion in downtown Ottawa. Sir Wilfrid Laurier lived there. He was our seventh prime minister, holding office from 1896 to 1911. Check him out on a five-dollar bill. His house was willed to Mackenzie King, who lived there from 1923 until his death in 1950. Mackenzie King, who never married and had no children, willed the house to the Canadian Crown. It was a contender for the permanent official residence of the prime minister, but Louis St. Laurent (he was our twelfth prime minister, from 1948 to 1957, please do keep up) opposed it. Instead, 24 Sussex Drive was designated as the prime minister's official residence in 1951. Laurier House is a designated National Historic Site.

A 1902 shot of Mackenzie King's old haunt, Laurier House.

• • • • • • • • • • • • • • • •

2. Whom did the grandson of Sir Arthur Conan Doyle's mystic pen pal play in *Ghostbusters*?

Answer: b) Raymond "Ray" Stantz

Mystic/dentist Samuel Aykroyd begat Peter Aykroyd, a civil engineer who worked as a policy adviser to Prime Minister Pierre Trudeau. Peter Aykroyd begat Dan Aykroyd, who co-wrote and starred in *Ghostbusters* as Raymond "Ray" Stantz. Dan Aykroyd's belief in spiritualism was a major inspiration for the script.

• • • • • • • • • • • • • • •

3. How many university degrees did Mackenzie King earn?

Answer: d) five

Mackenzie King earned five university degrees: a Bachelor of Arts in 1895, a Bachelor of Laws in 1896, and a Master of Arts in 1897, all from the University of Toronto, followed by a Master of Arts in political economy in 1898 and a Doctorate of Philosophy in 1908, both from Harvard. He is the only Canadian prime minister to hold a doctorate.

• • • • • • • • • • • • • • •

4. I was really hoping this chapter would have a connection to Lorne Greene. Does it?

Answer: a) yes

Angus McLellan, the CBC Radio producer who asked the spirit of Mackenzie King about the Canadian scene, studied at the Academy of Radio Arts in Toronto founded by Lorne Greene and then became head writer for Greene's daily newscasts on Toronto's CKEY/590 AM.

15

STEPHEN HARPER: HOCKEY FAN, *MURDOCH MYSTERIES* STAR

Much has been made of Prime Minister Pierre Trudeau's sense of style. He drove a sporty white convertible Mercedes-Benz 300SL Roadster, he installed a swanky swimming pool at 24 Sussex, and he rocked a cape, not at the National Arts Centre, but at that macho sports festival of normcore, the Grey Cup.

Even if you're not a fan of his politics, if you were asked to name a Canadian prime minister who had style, flair, and a sense of image, you'd probably name Trudeau (or his equally

Pierre Trudeau: swagger personified.

had that whole air of spiritual mystery surrounding him. Jean Chrétien is probably not top of mind unless you admire the fineness of his Shawinigan Handshake. And way down on the bottom of the list, even below Joe Clark, is Stephen Harper.

Harper was the twenty-second prime minister of Canada, serving from 2006 to 2015. His Lego-man hair, sweater vests, and pervasive blandness betray a man who made more out of his image than any of his predecessors.

His first opportunity to project his personal style on the nation came in 1978 when, as a high schooler, he made an appearance on CBC TV's academic teen quiz show *Reach for the Top* (or just *Reach*, as the cool kids call it). Although his team was trounced 445–160, Harper can take pride in the fact that he scored half of his foursome's points and

charismatic son, Prime Minister Justin Trudeau).

Beyond the Trudeaus, well, Lester B. Pearson could really wear a spiffy bow tie, Wilfrid Laurier was a silver fox, Mackenzie Bowell's facial hair was beyond reproach, and William Lyon Mackenzie King was brave enough to wear plaid bell-bottoms. Courage is a much sought-after quality in a leader.

He didn't really hold the attention of the nation again until the 2006 election campaign. Dubbed by the press as "the nerd who came from nowhere," he campaigned in a traditional suit and tie befitting the capital-C Conservative, capital-C Christian man he is. His appearance was cardboard-y, his speech delivery fluctuated between monotonous and robotic, and his absolute admonition of any lust for life rivalled that of Ned Flanders. He didn't have great style; he had *a* style.

And *a* style doesn't just come out of the ether. Harper knew this. That's why, when he took office in 2006, he became the first prime minister of Canada to hire a full-time stylist. Let's be clear: This was not an economic stylist or a policy stylist or a tin-man oil-application stylist. Those are imaginary things that don't exist. Harper hired a *stylist*-stylist. Yes. The ones that do hair, makeup, and wardrobe. Yes. She was a professional with credentials and references. Yes, what we see when we see Harper is the "after" shot, not the "before."

Take some time to let this settle. Look out the window and shake your head slowly and gently while trying to come to terms. Take a deep, cleansing breath. The taxpayers paid her salary. Just keep breathing. In and out. You're doing great.

The issue of stylist Michelle Muntean's salary was raised in the House of Commons, which gave Labrador Liberal MP Todd Russell the chance to unleash this zinger: "Canadians speculated for months whether the PM was sporting enough eyeliner to make an eighties rock band proud."

The vest.

The government shut out repeated questions about who paid Muntean's salary and what her salary amounted to and what was wrong with her eyesight/judgment. In mid-2007, the source of Muntean's salary was switched from the public purse to tax-deductible donations to the Conservative Party. Muntean, the cowlick whisperer charged with keeping the prime minister's mascara subtle, even travelled with him to choose his suits and ties and do his hair and face. She was presumably on hand at the 2005 Calgary Stampede where Harper disastrously donned a too-tight black leather vest. One imagines her contribution was to advise him against wearing the matching chaps.

But a high-profile guy has got to do whatever it takes to look his best, and Harper was high profile. In addition to running the country, he made a cameo appearance on the hit Saskatchewan-set sitcom *Corner Gas* in 2007. In 2009, he joined internationally renowned cellist Yo-Yo Ma on stage at a National Arts Centre gala where he performed "With a Little Help from My Friends" on piano. (Take a moment here to uncurl your toes.) He rang in 2010 in a Tim Hortons marketing team's wet dream: He interviewed Wayne Gretzky and Gordie Howe for a Kinsmen Club of Saskatoon charity event.

And then he hit the big time. *Murdoch Mysteries* is one of television's most successful and longest-running shows. The Canadian program is based on the novels of Toronto author Maureen Jennings and is broadcast in more than one hundred countries. Harper never misses an episode. In October of 2010, he had the opportunity to play the small role

Harper loves his hockey. In the top pic, he cheers on Team Canada vs. Team Russia during the gold medal game of the IIHF World Junior Championships in 2015. Canada won 5–4. Below, we see him at game four of the Western Conference quarter-finals between the Anaheim Ducks and Winnipeg Jets during the 2015 NHL Stanley Cup Playoffs in Winnipeg.

of Desk Sergeant Armstrong on the Victorian-era crime drama. It was the first time a sitting prime minister had taken on an acting role. In his scene, Armstrong disagrees with Murdoch's sidekick, Crabtree, about the Ottawa hockey team's playoff prospects, whereupon Crabtree tells him he doesn't know the first thing about hockey. The pair's hot-stove chat is interrupted when the prime minister arrives, asking for Murdoch. Armstrong asks him, "And you would be?" before Crabtree admonishes him for not recognizing Sir Wilfred Laurier.

Harper, who's famously hockey-crazed, spent his spare time while in office writing *A Great Game: The Forgotten Leafs and the Rise of Professional Hockey*, which was released in 2013. Don't worry; it's not all faced-paced action. If you were hoping to read about the development of artificial ice rinks in the early twentieth century, this book has the answers you crave. The *National Post* called it "a savagely dull tome … He says he wrote it himself, and I absolutely believe him."

Harsh reviews aside, how does a nerd from nowhere get so lucky? It's almost as though he was guided by mystic counsel. He was head of the country, appeared on his favourite TV show, and hung out with hockey legends. Could it be because his stylist was also a psychic? It's true. Although Harper's camp maintains that the prime minister didn't pay for clairvoyance services, there was no denial that Muntean was indeed a practising psychic. Maybe Harper didn't pay for readings because they were provided pro bono by his stylist. Or by the looks of things, Harper may very well have had a full-time psychic on the payroll

and the "stylist" title was a red herring to distract the Opposition and the media. At any rate, we'll find out the details when Harper's diary is published posthumously. Naturally, the CBC will produce and record a séance to contact him. Let's hope they ask him about the importance of image. In the meantime, here are some things I've been meaning to ask you:

• • • • • • • • • • • • • •

1. **What was Stephen Harper's first foray into public affairs?**
   a) his role as chief aide to Progressive Conservative MP Jim Hawkes
   b) his first federal election campaign
   c) his scientific investigation into the Great Canadian Flag Debate
   d) his term as Reform MP Deborah Grey's executive assistant

2. **Who has hosted *Reach for the Top*?**
   a) Alex Trebek
   b) Monty Hall
   c) Alan Thicke
   d) Howie Mandel
   e) all of the above

3. **In a 2007 Harris/Decima poll, what percentage of Canadian respondents agreed with the statement, "There is something about Stephen Harper that I just don't like."**
   a) 25 percent
   b) 35 percent
   c) 45 percent
   d) 55 percent
   e) all of the above

4. **How do you give a Shawinigan Handshake?**
   a) lick the back of your hand, then shake
   b) covertly tickle the other person's palm with your index or middle finger while shaking
   c) make the sign of the cross while reciting this verse:

   Saint Maurice in the crease
   His helmet made of hair grease
   Quick release, oh câlisse!
   It's Cataractes' masterpiece

   d) grab the other person's neck in a non-playful fashion

ANSWERS

· · · · · · · · · · · · · · · ·
1. What was Stephen Harper's first foray into public affairs?

Answer: c) his scientific investigation into the Great Canadian Flag Debate

Harper became chief aide to Progressive Conservative MP Jim Hawkes in 1985. He got his first taste of federal election campaigns during his losing bid to become MP for Calgary West in 1988. On the ballot, his name appeared as "Steve Harper" (who was probably a really cool guy). In 1989, Reform MP Deborah Grey was elected to Parliament and Harper became her executive assistant, chief adviser, and speechwriter until 1993. But Harper's very first foray into public affairs came in 1964 when he polled everyone on his street regarding their views on the divisive issue of the best design for Canada's new flag. He was five at the time, and the winning design was raised outside his kindergarten classroom.

· · · · · · · · · · · · · · · ·
2. Who has hosted *Reach for the Top*?

Answer: a) Alex Trebek

Best known as the host of *Jeopardy!* for more than thirty years, Sudbury, Ontario–born Alex Trebek acted as quizmaster on *Reach for the Top* from 1966 to 1973. Winnipeg's Monty Hall hosted *Let's Make A Deal* for nearly twenty years. Best known as the dad on *Growing Pains* and the dad to singer Robin Thicke, Alan Thicke of Kirkland Lake, Ontario, hosted the *Match Game Hollywood Squares Hour* in 1984. Toronto stand-up comedian

Howie Mandel hosted *Deal or No Deal* from 2005 to 2009.

. . . .

3. In a 2007 Harris/Decima poll, what percentage of Canadian respondents agreed with the statement, "There is something about Stephen Harper that I just don't like."

Answer: d) 55 percent

A majority of Canadians agreed that there was something about the leader that was just plum unlikeable. If you guessed e) all of the above, please be advised that these quizzes are not designed as a drinking game.

. . . .

4. How do you give a Shawinigan Handshake?

Answer: d) grab the other person's neck in a non-playful fashion

"Shawinigan Handshake" is the sobriquet given to the chokehold that then prime minister Jean Chrétien administered to protester Bill Clennett at the 1996 Flag Day ceremonies in Hull, Quebec. During his address, the prime minister had been heckled by a small group of anti-poverty activists in reaction to proposed changes to unemployment insurance. When Chrétien headed to his car after the event, Clennett got in his face. Chrétien, who was born in Shawinigan, Quebec, as the eighteenth of nineteen children, is known for standing up for himself. He grabbed Clennett by the neck and threw him to the ground. Even though the assault caused him to break a tooth, Clennett didn't press charges. For his part, Chrétien blamed the RCMP for letting Clennett get up in his grill. He later joked that he had mistaken Clennett for John

Nunziata, the York South-Weston MP whom Chrétien had expelled from the Liberal caucus because he voted against the budget in protest of the government's broken promise to rescind the GST.

Shawinigan Handshake is also the name of a hops-forward wheat beer that's been brewed in Chrétien's hometown by *Le Trou du Diable* microbrewery since 2010. The label depicts our twentieth prime minister giving a Shawinigan Handshake to the devil. In an alternate label design created to commemorate the 2012 Memorial Cup, he's choking out hockey commentator Don Cherry. "Don Cherry had loved it that I grabbed a protester by the neck," Chrétien, who is a fan of the brew, told the *Canadian Press*. "So I said, 'It's your turn, you will be the victim of that,' and he has accepted." What a marvellous image.

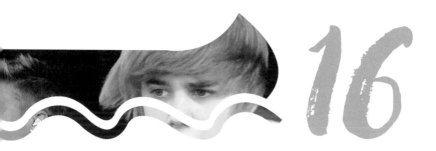

JUSTIN TRUDEAU:
#HAIR

On July 23, 1971, Prime Minister Pierre Trudeau's office issued a formal announcement that his wife, Margaret Trudeau, was expecting a baby.

When Pierre Trudeau had risen to power in '69, the *Vancouver Sun* had described

him as "a swinging bachelor." Although notoriously private about his personal life, he was soon in a high-profile relationship with American superstar Barbra Streisand. So it was a shock when, on March 5, 1971, front-page headlines across the nation proclaimed that Trudeau had suddenly married a twenty-two-year-old Vancouver woman while he was meant to be on a skiing holiday. The stunning announcement marked the end of the fifty-one-year-old's bachelor days. It wasn't a snap decision on the couple's part, though. They had dated casually since 1968, and wedding plans had been covertly undertaken by Trudeau's principal secretary, Marc Lalonde.

And now, less than five months after the surprise wedding, the nation's imagination was captured by the notion of the glamorous newlyweds' first child. On Parliament Hill, betting pools were established for the birthdate. Tickets were available for a dollar.

The birth of Justin Trudeau on Christmas Day, 1971, made international headlines. Newspapers around the world carried the official photo of the newborn Trudeau held lovingly by his mother.

On his way in to visit his wife at Ottawa Civic Hospital on Monday, December 27, *Père Pierre* passed out cigars to the reporters and photographers camped outside. "I'm afraid he looks like me," he told them. "Was he born with much hair?" the press asked. "About as much as me," said the balding prime minister. Justin Trudeau was two days old when the nation's long-held fascination with his hair began.

By the time the writ was dropped for the 2015 federal election, a forty-four-year-old Justin Trudeau had followed in his father's footsteps to become leader of the Liberal Party. He prepared to square off against political rivals Thomas Mulcair of the New Democratic Party (NDP) and Stephen Harper, the incumbent Conservative prime minister.

The kid has such great hair he can even rock a bowl cut.

But ever since Trudeau had won the Liberal leadership two years prior, the media had been amping up its focus on his hair. The *Huffington Post Canada* was a pioneer in this brand of coverage with its April 2013 article, "Justin Trudeau Style: His Hair Evolution." "We are keen to see whether Pierre Trudeau has passed off any of his stylish genes to his son," the news site wrote. The senior Trudeau's personal style was a major factor in inspiring the circa-'68 bout of Trudeaumania that helped usher him into power. The *Huffington Post*'s conclusion was that Justin Trudeau's wavy auburn mane was "basically perfect." Sure, *HuffPo*'s coverage could be considered fluff and not the sort of hard news an authoritative international magazine like, say, *The Economist* would run. But two weeks before the election, *The Economist* ran a profile of Trudeau's chances of succeeding his father under the uncharacteristically punny headline "Hair Apparent."

Much of the renewed focus on Trudeau's 'do stemmed from a Conservative Party political TV ad that launched in May 2015 and aimed to convince voters that Trudeau wasn't ready for the job. In the commercial, titled "The Interview," a group of office workers meet to mull over a job candidate's qualifications and take turns cattily tearing apart the Liberal leader's resume. "I see he's included his picture," one woman says derisively. Another guy pipes up to say "Legalizing marijuana? Is that the biggest problem we have to solve?" as a heady section

of the nation, watching from their couches as the ad interrupts their afternoon stories or late-night talk shows, screams "YES" in unison at the television each time the ad airs. The office group seems to take pleasure in tearing down Trudeau's perceived lack of experience, judgment, and knowledge. "Nice hair, though," a man says at the end. He says it in a way that should have spawned a national conversation about the ridiculously poor quality of the acting in Conservative ads. Instead, hair became an election issue.

In the *New York Times*, Vanessa Friedman wrote, "Hair has not played such a big part in a political contest as far back as I can remember. It puts the flurry of conversation around Hillary Rodham Clinton's do-switcheroos, John Edwards's $400 cut, and Mitt Romney's crowning glory in the shade."

Trudeau's hair got its own unauthorized parody Twitter account, @TrudeausHair. A typical tweet asked, "Ready for leadership you just want to run your fingers through? I'm ready to deliver. #elxn42 #naturallycurly."

Realizing that hair had become a potentially legitimate election determinant, NDP candidate Mulcair's team worked up an official line of memorabilia capitalizing on his beard. In a real, actual political election campaign *in our nation, in our time*, a major party candidate passed out pin-back buttons inviting voters to "beard part of it" and posters declaring "I'm voting for the beard."

Eventually, esteemed Canadian poet and novelist Margaret Atwood could not resist delivering her take on the matter. She penned a *National Post* column entitled, "Hair is in the election-season air, but is it crucial

Thomas Mulcair, a.k.a "the Beard."

to the question of your vote?" After chiding the Conservatives for raising the issue of a candidate's hair after it was made public that Harper employs an image consultant at the public's expense, Atwood wondered, "Will the Conservatives now lay off on the personal-appearance attack stuff? Doubtful: they've got a thing for it. Jean Chrétien's paralyzed face, laugh a minute! Trudeau's hair, woo-woo! Who's next? 'Nice tits, Elizabeth [May]?'"

Just before Atwood distracted us with language at which parents would shake their heads, she referenced the 1993 federal election campaign. That year, the Conservatives ran an attack ad against Liberal leader Jean Chrétien that showed a series of unflattering close-up photos of his face. Chrétien had been bullied as a child because an attack of Bell's palsy had left him partially deaf and with the left side of his face partially paralyzed; critics accused the Conservatives of using Chrétien's appearance and health condition against him. So, on the bright side of things, "The Interview" ad marked a move toward more civilized attack ads on behalf of Stephen Harper's party. "Nice hair, though," is technically a compliment.

Now, which of these quiz answers are technically correct?

1. **Pierre Trudeau was the first Canadian prime minister to father a child in office since**
   a) Sir John A. Macdonald
   b) Louis St. Laurent
   c) Arthur Meighen
   d) Robert Borden

2. **Whose hair cuttings are worth $40,000?**
   a) Justin Trudeau
   b) Justin Timberlake
   c) Justin Bieber
   d) Justin Morneau

3. **True or False: Justin Trudeau and Stephen Harper have the same hairdresser.**

4. **How much does Justin Trudeau pay for a haircut?**
   a) $40
   b) $140
   c) $240
   d) $400

ANSWERS

. . . .

1. Pierre Trudeau was the first Canadian prime minister to father a child in office since

Answer: a) Sir John A. Macdonald

Justin Trudeau was just the second child in Canadian history to be born to a prime minister in office. The first was Sir John A. Macdonald's daughter, Mary, who was born on February 8, 1869.

. . . .

2. Whose hair cuttings are worth $40,000?

Answer: c) Justin Bieber

On the eve of her 2011 birthday, talk show host Ellen DeGeneres tweeted: "It's my birthday tomorrow! All I want for my birthday is world peace, and a lock of @JustinBieber's hair." The following month, Bieber delivered. During an appearance on her show, he presented her with a box of trimmings from a recent cut.

Other hair from that cut was donated to Bieber's fave charity, Pencils of Promise. They sold the hair to Paul Fraser Collectibles in exchange for enough money to build a school.

The Paul Fraser Collectibles website is an absurd delight. In the market for Gandhi's bowl, spoon, and fork? Paul Fraser's got you covered. Hoping to pick up Einstein's leather jacket? Look no further. Authentic strands of hair go for £399 on the Bristol, U.K.–based site, the equivalent of about $525 Canadian. They offer authentic single strands of hair from notables as diverse as Marilyn Monroe, John Adams, Geronimo, Sir Paul McCartney,

PaulFraser Collectibles

Home   Buy   Layaway plan   Sell   Investing   Free Newsletter

Home > Buy > Famous Hair >

Justin Bieber Authentic Hair Cuttings

Justin Bieber Authentic Hair Cuttings

For Sale: £35,000.00

Justin Bieber's hair from his famous haircut – the ultimate piece of Justin Bieber merchandise

In February 2011 teen sensation Justin Bieber had a famous haircut.

Justin gave some of the clippings to TV star Ellen Degeneres after she tweeted "All I want for my birthday is a lock of Justin Bieber's hair".

Ellen sold the Justin Bieber hair on Ebay for $40,668, with the proceeds going towards her favourite charity, The Gentle Barn. The hair was purchased by the Golden Palace Casino and now forms part of their travelling museum of weird and wonderful merchandise.

Justin donated the rest of the hair to his favourite charity, Pencils of Promise. They in turn contacted Paul Fraser Collectibles and we acquired the hair in return for a considerable donation that is to be used to build a new school in the developing world.

The hair is presented in a plastic container which has been initialled by Justin Bieber himself. There are approximately 200 one inch hairs in total.

Justin Bieber's hair built a school.

Charles Dickens, Bieber, Hans Christian Andersen, Neil Armstrong, Napoleon, Elvis Presley, and George Washington.

In addition to offering single strands of official Bieber hair at the going rate, Paul Fraser also offers what looks like a gross little pill bottle with Bieber's initials scribbled on the lid. Inside are 200 strands of the pop star's hair. It's available for £35,000 (about $60,266 Canadian). It's an amazing price. Think about it: If you bought all those strands individually at £399, you'd be spending a whopping £79,800 ($137,408 Canadian). You're practically saving money in this deal. Really, you can't afford *not* to buy it.

What makes Bieber's hair worth the price? Canada's second most-powerful Justin was born in 1994 to no international fanfare. His unwed mother was a teen and his father was in jail. Unlike Justin Trudeau, who grew up accompanying his father on trips to meet foreign dignitaries including the pope and once had to go home from school to have lunch with the Queen, Bieber was a regular kid who lived in low-income housing, played

"The Great Young": Bieber rocks a Gretzky jersey in 2016.

hockey, and learned to play piano, guitar, trumpet, and drums. His mom uploaded his music to YouTube, where he was noticed by a talent manager, which led to a record deal for the fifteen-year-old. Over the next seven years, he sold more than 45 million albums and became one of the most popular, influential, and wealthy stars of the century.

During Prime Minister Justin Trudeau's address at his 2016 state dinner at the White House, he broached the topic of international trade:

"Over $2.4 billion worth of goods and services cross the [Canada-U.S.] border every day — evidence of one of the largest and most mutually beneficial trading relationships in the world. And one of our most popular exports to the United States, and I need you to stop teasing him, has been another Justin. Now, no, no, that kid has had a great year. And of course, leave it to a Canadian to reach international fame with a song called 'Sorry.'"

The line drew guffaws and applause. Trudeau, a father of three, had made a dad joke that would make Sir John A. Macdonald proud.

How has Bieber managed to stay on top in the face of puberty, One Direction, and that thing where he pelted his neighbour's house with eggs and peed in a restaurant's mop bucket? "When he feels even a little bit like the world is starting to doubt him, he kicks into overdrive," his manager Scooter Braun told *Maclean's*. "He's very competitive — a Canadian hockey player at heart."

For his part, Bieber said, "I try to give a positive message. I say I'm on this stage and I never thought I could do this. Whether you want to be a doctor or an engineer, you just gotta have that motivation and you can do anything if you set your mind to it." This man cut off his hair and it paid for a school. What's not to beliebe?

• • • • • • • • • • • • • •

3. True or False: Justin Trudeau and Stephen Harper have the same hairdresser.

Answer: true

But how can this be so? In addition to his image consultant, Harper avails himself of the services of Ottawa hairdresser Stefania Capovilla. Trudeau's mother, Margaret, is a long-time client of Capovilla's; she even styled Maggie's hair for Trudeau's 2005 wedding to Sophie Grégoire. (That day, Trudeau and his bride left the church in the white convertible Mercedes-Benz 300SL Roadster he had inherited from his father.) Capovilla is the go-to hairdresser for the Parliament Hill set. In addition to clipping Harper and Trudeau, she has also maintained the manes of former Conservative Immigration Minister Jason Kenney, former Conservative Finance Minister Jim Flaherty and Senator Patrick Brazeau.

• • • • • • • • • • • • • •

4. How much does Justin Trudeau pay for a haircut?

Answer: a) $40

Like all of Stefania Capovilla's male clients, Trudeau pays $40 for a cut.

BONUS ROUND

Mascots

WHICH OF THESE CREATIONS
WERE BROUGHT TO FRUITION?

HIDY AND HOWDY: TWIN RODEO POLAR BEARS

The word *mascot* originates from the French word *mascotte*, which means "lucky charm." Popular mascots of the past have been objects like a horseshoe, the foot of what would seem to be a rather luckless rabbit, or even a loved one's lock of hair. Modern mascots are usually big furry animal suits worn by mute acrobats or professional huggers, and their role has been expanded from good luck charms to appropriately affectionate goodwill ambassadors.

Since 1968, the Olympic Games' host city has chosen a

mascot to represent its culture and values. When Calgary, Alberta, played to host the 1988 Winter Olympics, they had a myriad of animals to choose from.

Alberta is home to a marvellous menagerie of mammals. Elk meander at trailheads, signs of beavers can be seen on hiking trails, bighorn sheep gather roadside, and gopher-like ground squirrels pop up from their field burrows to issue a chipper "Peep-peep-peep!" Grizzly bears, foxes, caribou, brown bears, cougars, bison, bobcats, and more make this western province their home. But one mammal you won't see in the Sunshine Province is the polar bear.

So it would be ridiculous for a polar bear to represent the Calgary Olympics. That's probably why Calgary designer Sheila Scott doubled down and suggested that *two* polar bears act as mascots.

Hidy and Howdy say "Hi!" at the '87 Canada Cup in Calgary.

The Calgary Zoo, which is home to zero polar bears, sponsored a competition to name the polar bear pair. Calgary high school student Kim Johnstone's submission was selected from more than five thousand entries and, at her suggestion, the bears were christened Hidy and Howdy.

While "hidy" failed to catch on as a salutation, "howdy" has long been a common greeting among the cowboy set, making the name perfect to evoke Calgary, the Stampede City. Sure, a pair of horse mascots would also be a great fit, but that's a little on the nose. Better to outfit Hidy and Howdy in red-and-blue square-dancing costumes, with Hidy in a petticoat, puff-sleeved blouse, and bow and Howdy in a vest and neckerchief — *sans* pants, in the grand tradition of cartoon bears like Winnie the Pooh and Yogi Bear. As a nod to polar bears' natural penchant for Western-style headwear, both wore cowboy hats.

With Kindchenschema-inspired faces featuring big cheeks, a small nose and jaw, and large eyes set low on the face, Hidy and Howdy were designed for maximum cuteness.

Such hats! Our Olympic mascots raise the flag at Calgary City Hall in '84.

Experiments have demonstrated that seeing cute faces improves our concentration and hones our fine motor skills, a handy evolutionary trait that helps ensure we

a) handle babies carefully, and
b) are eager to hug a duo of bipedal *Ursidae* at a

pancake breakfast or sporting event.

Further scientific research has shown that seeing cute creatures makes our brains release dopamine, an important "feel-good" chemical. So in addition to prompting affection, Hidy and Howdy's cuteness factor was also important for merchandise sales. The Olympic mascot committee was, after all, comprised of reps from Calgary's major department stores, and it was important that Hasbro's official Hidy and Howdy dolls (as well as hundreds of other bits of memorabilia bearing the pair's likeness) be hot sellers at the Games.

The athletes' uniforms reflected Hidy and Howdy's dress sense of chilly rodeo chic. Here, Olympic silver medalist Brian Orser of Belleville, Ontario, flag-bears his way into the 1988 Olympics opening ceremony under a Howdy-style hat.

Hidy and Howdy made their international debut at the closing ceremonies of the Sarajevo Olympics in 1984. It was their first of about fifty thousand appearances over the twenty years that followed. Within the bear costumes was a pair of high school students. One hundred and thirty volunteer actors were recruited from Calgary's

Bishop Carroll High School to perform as Hidy and Howdy, wearing one of twenty-two sets of costumes. Although the bears are actually brother and sister and not a couple, the mascot program also recruited sixty chaperones.

In addition to a rule that is common to most mascots — no talking in costume — Hidy and Howdy couldn't hug anyone in a black suit because, while the fur of real polar bears is transparent, Hidy and Howdy's was white and prone to shedding.

In the lead-up to the Games, the bears were everywhere. They skated, skied, and zipped down the bobsleigh track. On a visit to Greece, Howdy received such an enthusiastic mauling by children that the front of his costume virtually disintegrated. On a trip to Toronto, they visited the children's hospital, where Hidy held the hand of a nine-year-old comatose boy who was not expected to revive. The child squeezed the bear's paw, opened his eyes and smiled. He passed later that day. No wonder the teens who'd played the mascot roles were heartbroken as the Games came to a close. Carolyn Symons, one of twelve original student performers, told the *Calgary Herald*, "It's going to be really sad, like losing a good friend."

The costumes, which were manufactured by the International Mascot Corporation in Edmonton, Alberta, were no doubt built to last, but according to International Olympic Committee protocol, mascots must be destroyed after the Games. At the time, mascot chairman Lane Kranenburg dismissed rumours that the bears would be put down, telling the

Hidy and Howdy chillin' in Canmore, Alberta.

Committee in Switzerland. Two other pairs survived to retire at the Canmore Museum and Geoscience Centre in Canmore, Alberta, and at Canada's Sports Hall of Fame in Calgary. The rest of the epically cute bear costumes were cut into pieces, which were given to the high school students who had brought them to life.

Herald, "We'll be sending them back home to the North Pole." As per tradition, a set of the mascot costumes was donated to the International Olympic

You might never be an epically cute bear or an Olympic champion, but you could still totally crush this quiz like a true Canadian winner:

1. **Which famous Canadian is an alumnus of Bishop Carroll High School?**

   a) singer/songwriter Feist

   b) WWE wrestler Natalya

   c) Alberta premier Alison Redford

   d) hockey legend Hayley Wickenheiser

   e) all of the above

2. **Canada's first Olympic mascot was a**

   a) beaver

   b) narwhal

   c) maple leaf

   d) whale

3. **Mascots are often chosen to reflect the predatory instinct of the team they represent. What percentage of polar bear hunts are successful?**

   a) more than 98 percent

   b) 53 percent

   c) 11 percent

   d) less than 2 percent

4. **A live raccoon was originally chosen as the mascot for the 1980 Winter Games in Lake Placid, New York, but he was replaced because**

   a) the U.S. Olympic Committee could not abide by a raccoon mascot

   b) he escaped

   c) no corporation would sponsor him

   d) he was deemed not cute enough

Answers

· · · · · · · · · · · · · · · ·

1. Which famous Canadian is an alumnus of Bishop Carroll High School?

Answer: e) all of the above

Natalie Katherine "Natalya" Neidhart is a member of the legendary Hart wrestling family who trained under the tutelage of her uncles, Ross and Bruce Hart. She was six years old when her hometown hosted the Olympics. In 2010, she won the WWE Divas Championship, then joined the cast of E!'s *Total Divas* reality show in 2013. Four-time Grammy nominee and ten-time JUNO winner Feist attended Bishop Carroll as well as Calgary's public Alternative High School, which sounds like the school all the cool kids went to in the '90s. At age twelve, she was one of a thousand dancers who wowed at the Calgary Winter Olympics opening ceremonies. Alison Redford was born in Kitimat, British Columbia, and lived in Nova Scotia and Borneo before settling in Calgary with her family at age twelve. After graduating from Bishop Carroll, she studied at the College of Law at the University of Saskatchewan, from which she graduated in 1988. Hayley Wickenheiser is widely considered the best female hockey player in the world. She has represented Canada at the Winter Olympics five times and has brought home four gold medals and a silver. She's won more gold than any other Canadian. She also competed in softball at the 2000 Summer Olympics in Sydney. In 2008, *Sports*

Superstar hockey champion Hayley Wickenheiser.

Illustrated named her number 20 in a list of the top 25 toughest athletes in the world. Wickenheiser was elected to the International Olympic Committee's Athletes' Commission in 2014.

• • • • • • • • • • • • • • •

2. Canada's first Olympic mascot was a

Answer: a) beaver

In 1970, TVOntario began broadcasting, the Hudson's Bay Company moved its headquarters from London, England, to Winnipeg, Manitoba, and the CRTC issued its first Canadian content rules for radio and television. In May of that year, five months before the FLQ crisis cast a pall across the nation, Montreal was awarded the 1976 Olympic Summer Games.

The mascot was a beaver named Amik. In the Anishinaabe language, *amik* means beaver, so for those who are English/Anishinaabe bilingual, his name was Beaver the Beaver (or Amik the Amik). The sleek Amik was a feat of design and an afterthought for retailers. No furry

Montréal 1976

pantomime beaver costumes of Amik were manufactured, but his quiet, sophisticated simplicity is the triumphant antithesis of the garish 1996 Atlanta Summer Games mascot, Izzy, which Bob Costas called "a genetic experiment gone horribly, ghastly wrong."

3. **Mascots are often chosen to reflect the predatory instinct of the team they represent. What percentage of polar bear hunts are successful?**

Answer: d) less than 2 percent

Despite their ferocious reputation as the most predatory, carnivorous member of the bear family, most Arctic land animals can outrun polar bears and most marine creatures can out-swim them. Luckily, polar bears can fast for several months at a time even though they don't technically hibernate (unless they're knocked up).

4. **A live raccoon was originally chosen as the mascot for the 1980 Winter Games in Lake Placid, New York, but he was replaced because**

Answer: c) no corporation would sponsor him

In 1978, a five-month-old raccoon wearing a T-shirt emblazoned with the Olympic logo was unveiled as the Games' official mascot. In between press conferences, fundraisers, and appearances on *Good Morning America* and *The Tonight Show*, he lived with his sister at the Utica City Zoo.

In 1980, he was dumped in favour of a teen in a polyester raccoon costume sponsored by Coca-Cola. "We couldn't find a corporate sponsor for the live raccoon," press spokesman Thomas Johnson of the Lake Placid Olympic Organizing Committee told the *Poughkeepsie Journal*. Johnson was delighted by the replacement. "We used him at a big fundraiser we had at the Xenon discotheque in New York City. He discoed all over the floor. He was just perfect. There are just some things he can do that little animals can't."

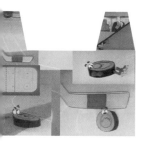

18

PETER PUCK: THE *ITCHY & SCRATCHY* OF HOCKEY

At the start of the 1974 debut episode of *Peter Puck*, our cheerful, animated puck buddy establishes the theme:

"This time I'm going to tell you about playing the game." *Whack!* "NHL hockey, that is! The world's fastest team sport." *Whack!*

Yes, Peter Puck, our happy host, has just been whacked across the ice repeatedly by hockey sticks. Imagine watching Mickey Mouse get hit with a hammer mid-monologue. It's unexpected and not unenjoyable. It's invigorating, thrilling even. But not because Peter Puck is annoying. Quite the opposite. He is simple and charming, not cloying at all, which is a rare achievement for a wisdom-imparting animated character (just ask the many enemies made by Clippy, the much-loathed cartoon paperclip that acted as a helper in '90s-era Microsoft Office software).

Peter Puck was created by NBC Sports executive producer Scotty Connal and NBC executive Donald Carswell to help popularize hockey by explaining it to new and young viewers. The character himself is charming, but the sheer number of facts, figures, definitions, terms, and regulations he quickly imparts in a crusade to bring newbies up to speed with the rules of hockey sure feels a lot like learning. And just as this realization begins to dawn on the viewer, *whack!* Down the ice he goes.

Much of the show's magnetism comes from the tension created by the visual cuteness of the character, the resentment of being tricked into learning, and the catharsis of seeing this sneaky teacher being thwacked repeatedly. We also see him, hypothermic, in the freezer pre-game. "That's to take a little bit of the bounce out of my hard rubber body!" he explains.

The series was produced by Hanna-Barbera, the same animation company behind the sadistic adventures of Tom and Jerry. The studio was known to employ the cost-saving technique of limited animation, but for a company known for its slapdash procedure, they really outdid themselves during a segment that explains how skates are made by presenting a detailed animated visual of industrial manufacturing processes that looks like a cartoon episode of *How It's Made*. Stick and puck manufacturing are given the same treatment. Soon after *Peter Puck*'s debut, Connal claimed it was the most popular segment of their coverage during intermissions.

Peter Puck's design is simple — he's a cartoon puck with those expressive, disembodied eyebrows that wiggle in the air above his head. His red skates float below, and red gloves hover at his sides. When not imparting knowledge, he issues mild complaints as he's shot around the rink, such as, "Easy does it, fellas, this is only a demonstration!" and, "Oh, why didn't I listen to my mother and become a bicycle tire or an eraser?"

The hockey players are depicted as the NHL brass probably sees them: simple, indistinguishable, lantern-jawed hunks of meat whose words are as unintelligible as those of Charlie Brown's teacher. Since the NHL didn't introduce helmet rules until 1979, the players here wear no helmets, and they probably think less of the goalie for wearing that mask. The star here — and you can tell, because he's the only one who has pupils drawn in his eyes — is Peter Puck.

When they stopped carrying NHL games in 1975, NBC sold the character's rights back to Hanna-Barbera, who in turn sold them to Brian McFarlane, a commentator on CBC's flagship sports broadcast, *Hockey Night in Canada,* who'd had a hand in Peter Puck's creation, even flying to Hollywood to coach Hanna-Barbera's animation specialists in the creation process. Born in New Liskeard, Ontario, in 1931, McFarlane was raised in Ottawa and Whitby, where he played hockey well enough to earn a university scholarship to New York State. After graduation, he pursued a career in

Most Canadian photo ever? A child shares ice cream with Peter Puck in front of a chip wagon with poutine on the menu. In the background is Canada's first parliamentary building in Kingston, Ontario.

broadcasting and joined *HNIC* as a commentator in 1964. McFarlane has written nearly one hundred books on hockey, including the three children's books *Peter Puck: Love That Hockey Game!* in 1975, 1980's *Peter Puck and the Stolen Stanley Cup*, and *Peter Puck's Greatest Moments in Hockey*.

After that, Peter Puck quietly retired. But in a comeback that could rival Mario Lemieux's, he re-emerged in 2007 to ride the retro revivalism wave right back into our frozen rubber hearts.

The new Peter Puck episodes move faster, with quick edits, and run for a third of the time of the original episodes' three minutes. Despite the 3D animation, the character retains his charm and simplicity. Episodes are less educational and more focused on superstar players. Peter Puck still gets full concussions in every episode. It's the most violent cartoon on the air today, save *Itchy & Scratchy*. In one recent reel, he's dinged off the goalpost and thinks he's seeing double, which leads tidily into a profile of the Vancouver Canucks' Sedin twins. His latest book, *Peter Puck's Big Book of Hockey: Fascinating Facts for Hockey Fans of All Ages*, hit shelves in 2010.

And now here are some quiztastic fascinating facts for you:

• • • • • • • • • • • • • •

1. **Which '60s music star provided the voice of Peter Puck in the original series?**

   a) Micky Dolenz of the Monkees

   b) Denny Doherty of The Mamas & the Papas

   c) Sylvia Tyson of Ian & Sylvia

   d) Lorne Greene, the man behind the 1964 smash hit "Ringo"

• • • • • • • • • • • • • •

2. **Who popularized the goalie mask?**

   a) Terry Sawchuk

   b) Jacques Plante

   c) Glenn Hall

   d) Lorne "Gump" Worsley

• • • • • • • • • • • • • •

3. **Which hockey players were also elected to provincial or federal parliament?**

   a) Ken Dryden and Red Kelly

   b) Syl Apps and Bucko McDonald

   c) Lionel Conacher and Howie Meeker

   d) all of the above

• • • • • • • • • • • • • •

4. **Brian McFarlane has written a series of charming books about Peter Puck. Which series of books did his father write?**

   a) The Chronicles of Narnia

   b) The Hardy Boys

   c) The Famous Five

   d) Clifford the Big Red Dog

Answers

• • • • • • • • • • • • • •

1. Which '60s music star provided the voice of Peter Puck?

Answer: a) Micky Dolenz of the Monkees

The original Peter Puck cartoon was voiced by Micky Dolenz of the Monkees and actor Ronnie Schell.

Bieber haircuts for everyone! The Monkees, featuring Micky Dolenz (top right), who was the voice of Peter Puck.

• • • • • • • • • • • • • •

2. Who popularized the goalie mask?

Answer: b) Jacques Plante

A consummate tough guy from Shawinigan, Quebec, Jacques Plante was one of the NHL's all-time greatest goalies, and he could have no doubt administered the Shawinigan Handshake with a flair to rival Chrétien's. But like Drake, by going against the game's macho grain and showing his vulnerability, he made his biggest contribution.

As immortalized in a 1991 *Heritage Minute*, a powerful slapshot broke Plante's nose early in a New York game in 1959, necessitating 200 stitches to his face. Plante refused to finish the game without his mask, which had been a fixture for him in practices for four years. He overcame the objections of his coach and the heckling of the crowd to wear his goalie mask and help his team win the game 3–1. It was the beginning of an eleven-game winning streak in a season that culminated with a Stanley Cup win, the last of Plante's six championship victories.

Plante was a resourceful crafter who not only made his own goalie masks, but also cooked, sewed, embroidered, and even knit his own toques and jerseys as an amateur player. He invented and constantly improved different styles of masks for himself and fellow players.

In the *Heritage Minute*, Plante is portrayed by Jason Cavalier, best known for his starring role as Mickey in *Time of Your Life*, a 1988 daily syndicated teen soap opera that laid the groundwork for *Degrassi: The Next Generation*.

• • • • • • • • • • • • • • •

3. Which hockey players were also elected to federal or provincial office?

Answer: d) all of the above

Hockey Hall of Fame goalie and Montreal Canadiens legend Ken Dryden was a member of the House of Commons for York Centre from 2004 to 2011. Red Kelly, who won the Lady Byng Trophy four times as the NHL's most gentlemanly player, was elected to the House of Commons in 1962 to represent the York West riding as one of Lester B. Pearson's Liberals. Olympic pole-vaulter and Maple Leafs centre Syl Apps left the NHL in 1948 after a twelve-year stint. He was a Progressive Conservative member of Ontario's provincial parliament for Kingston from 1963 to 1975. Three-time

Stanley Cup champion and Canadian Lacrosse Hall of Famer Bucko McDonald was a Liberal candidate elected to the House of Commons to represent the riding of Parry Sound, Ontario. Grey Cup winner and two-time Stanley Cup champ Lionel Conacher was elected to the Legislative Assembly of Ontario in 1937, representing the then riding of Bracondale in Toronto. Leafs right-winger Howie Meeker was the last surviving member of the Maple Leafs' 1947 Stanley Cup team; he spent two years as the Progressive Conservative MP for Waterloo South while playing in the NHL. What did *you* do after work today?

. . . .

4. Brian McFarlane has written a series of charming books about Peter Puck. Which series of books did his father write?

Answer: b) The Hardy Boys

Brian McFarlane's father, Leslie McFarlane, wrote twenty-one books in the bestselling Hardy Boys mystery series under the pseudonym Franklin W. Dixon.

McFarlane earned as little as $85 per book during the Great Depression and received no royalties on the series. Brian McFarlane told the *Globe and Mail*, "In his diaries my father talks about having to write another of those cursed books in order to earn another $100 to buy coal for the furnace. And he never read them over afterward. It was only much later that he accepted plaudits for the work."

McFarlane also worked for the National Film Board of Canada, writing and directing documentaries, including the 1953 film on Montreal Canadiens star Jean Beliveau, *Here's Hockey!* A friend of Lorne Greene, he also worked as a scriptwriter on the 1960s TV hit *Bonanza.* If you look hard enough, like a silver lining, Lorne Greene is always there.

19

YOUPPI!
THE ULTIMATE
FREE AGENT

Roger D. Landry was the assistant director of public relations for Montreal's epically successful Expo 67 World's Fair. He was the vice-president of marketing for the Montreal Expos. He spent two decades at the helm of the Montreal daily *La Presse*. He's a companion of the Order of Canada who has received multiple honourary doctorates. Landry is a man of many accomplishments who has had an immeasurable impact on his province and his country. Yet by far, the most dazzling aspect of his legacy is Youppi!,

A real catch: Youppi! plays catch during the 2002 MLB All-Star Game Home Run Derby.

the six-and-a-half-foot orange Muppet-y team mascot who winsomely slid across the dugout and into our national psyche.

As part of his marketing role with the Expos, Landry commissioned Bonnie Erickson to create a team mascot in the vein of Philadelphia's Phillie Phanatic, which she'd designed the previous year. Philadelphia fans had embraced the Phanatic against all odds: these same hardened fans had pelted Santa with snowballs during his stop at Veterans Stadium and were rumoured to have booed the Easter Bunny. But they were not immune to the silly and irreverent charms of a furry, green, duck-butted trumpet-face.

The '79 season saw the Expos welcome Youppi!, which is French for "yippee!" His name is always spelled with an exclamation point. His jersey number is an exclamation point. This entity is a waddling, arm-flailing, googly-eyed symbol of excitement. From the moment that he threw out the first pitch of the club's home opener, Youppi! was a hit.

He spawned endless merchandising opportunities, including plush dolls, pin-back buttons, bobbleheads, trading cards, piggy banks, hockey pucks, throw blankets, puppets, postcards, camping chairs, posters, and a set of figurines available exclusively at Gulf gas stations. Youppi! had hit the big time.

In 1982, his team gifted him a three-wheeled ATV with which to zip around the field. The following year, a fifteen-year-old performed "O Canada" at

We've reached peak Quebecois: Youppi! emerges from poutine on a *petit gâteau*.

Olympic Stadium. When she finished, the then little-known Celine Dion planted a kiss on Youppi!'s nose. Along with the Phillie Phanatic and the San Diego Padres' Famous Chicken, Youppi! is one of only three mascots ever to be inducted (informally) into the Baseball Hall of Fame.

But the good times couldn't last. In a 1989 game against the

Los Angeles Dodgers, Youppi! leaped onto the roof of the visitors' dugout. Dodgers manager Tommy Lasorda complained to the umpires, and Youppi! became the first mascot ever to be ejected from a game. *Globe and Mail* sports writer Allen Abel called Youppi! a "Quebec union man down to his orange skin" because he hid inside when *il pleut*. And then, on September 29, 2004, an unthinkable horror: the Expos played their final game in Montreal.

At the end of the season, the Expos baseball franchise moved to Washington, D.C., and was renamed the Nationals. Thirty-six years of Expos history and memorabilia were divided among the Canadian Baseball Hall of Fame, Panthéon des Sports du Québec, Cinémathèque Québécoise, and the McCord Museum. The Panthéon got Youppi!'s ATV and a bronze bust of Jackie Robinson.

The Expos had initially promised to bring Youppi! with them, but they soon reneged and adopted a new mascot, a bald eagle named Screech. Youppi! had been replaced by an American cliché designed by a nine-year-old who said that Screech was "strong and eats almost everything."

Youppi! had been abandoned. The *Globe and Mail* mused that a mascot is not a mascot without a team. The entire existential existence of Youppi! became a topic of national conversation. At kitchen tables, hands were wrung as parents tried to explain the beloved mascot's fate to their children. Tim Hortons–based debates broke out over whether Youppi! could ever represent Montreal's CFL team, the Alouettes, or if their lark-related team name

YOUPPI!

Is Youppi! even real?

would forever evoke the horror of backstabber birds like Screech.

Finally, on September 16, 2005, our long national nightmare came to an end. The Montreal Canadiens, the most storied franchise in Canadian sports history, announced that they were adopting Youppi! He would become the ninety-six-year-old organization's first-ever official mascot. The Habs family welcomed

243

Youppi!'s new fan family.

our furry hero with open arms.

The Bell Centre didn't just provide Youppi! with a new home — it installed an elaborate Youppi!ville, with our hero mascot as mayor. It was a match made in heaven. No — even better — it was a match made in Montreal. Fans didn't just cheer, they absolutely exclaimed!

Now it's time to absolutely quiz!

244

1. True or false: Youppi! rode a mechanical bull at a popular Montreal night club after losing a bet to the host of *The Tonight Show*.

2. An unusual lobster was nicknamed after Youppi! because

   a) it was furry

   b) it was orange

   c) it could predict baseball wins

   d) it rode an ATV

3. How much money did the San Diego Padres' Famous Chicken reportedly earn in 1985?

   a) $1

   b) $75,000

   c) $125,000

   d) $250,000

4. Youppi! designer Bonnie Erickson also created

   a) the town of Erickson, Manitoba

   b) Maplelea Girls dolls

   c) Miss Piggy

   d) the ookpik

ANSWERS

. . . .

1. True or false: Youppi! rode a mechanical bull at a popular Montreal night club after losing a bet to the host of *The Tonight Show*.

Answer: true

On the eve of the Canadiens' series against the New York Rangers for the 2014 Eastern Conference Finals, Jimmy Fallon, the host of the New York–based *Tonight Show*, made a wager with the Montreal team. If the Habs won the series, Fallon would don their jersey for his monologue. If the Rangers won, Youppi! would have to wear a Rangers jersey around Montreal and post ten pictures of it on the Canadiens' Twitter feed.

The Rangers took the series in six games and in June a thoroughly despondent Youppi! wore the hated New York jersey. The worst insult was Fallon's name across the back and a number one where Youppi!'s exclamation point should be. The dejected mascot forlornly posed at Olympic Stadium, Mount Royal, alone on a merry-go-round at La Ronde Six Flags, sitting pensively on an Old Montreal cobblestone road, slouched outside the Oratoire Saint-Joseph, and beyond. The final image shows a non-jubilant Youppi! riding the mechanical bull at Montreal bar Chez Serge.

. . . .

2. An unusual lobster was nicknamed after Youppi! because

Answer: b) he was orange

A three-pound lobster rose to fame in 2011 because of a genetic defect that turned him orange.

He was discovered in the tank of a grocery store in Trois-Rivières, Quebec, where the staff named him Youppi! because of his distinctive colouring. He was later renamed Youpi (one p, no exclamation point) to avoid a possible trademark infringement.

According to marine experts, about one in ten million lobsters is orange, making them three times rarer even than blue lobsters. Upon Youpi's passing, he was feted in a year-long funeral where he lay in state to allow the public to pay their respects.

• • • • • • • • • • • • • • •

3. **How much money did the San Diego Padres' Famous Chicken reportedly earn in 1985?**

Answer: d) $250,000

London, Ontario–born Ted Giannoulas is the one and only Famous Chicken. He began wearing the suit as a radio station promotion in 1974, and the mascot's popularity soon eclipsed that of the station and then, nearly, the slumping Padres team itself. Giannoulas credits the goalie days of his youth with making him limber and loose enough to deliver the chicken's famous brand of physical comedy. The Philadelphia Phillies commissioned their Phanatic mascot in hopes of replicating the Famous Chicken's draw at their stadium.

• • • • • • • • • • • • • • •

4. **Youppi! designer Bonnie Erickson also created**

Answer: c) Miss Piggy

Youppi! was designed by Bonnie Erickson, formerly a designer for Muppet-master Jim Henson. Among her favourite creations are Statler and Waldorf, the two old guys who heckle the Muppets from their balcony perch, and Zoot, the blue-haired saxophonist for the Muppet band Electric Mayhem. Erickson designed and built one of the most famous Muppets, Miss Piggy, in 1974 for an early Muppets TV special. Erickson had also worked with Henson on building costumes for the *Sesame Street* ice show. She was a pioneer in creating elaborate costumes in which people could perform and even skate. With this in mind, it feels like Youppi! was always destined to hit the ice in Montreal. He had somehow ended up in a place for which he never knew he was perfectly built.

Erickson is a former town in Manitoba with a current population of about 500. It was established in 1905 as a rail station. The town is named after its post office, which was in turn named after its postmaster, E. Albert Erickson. Who knew postmasters could just name stuff after themselves?

Maplelea Girls were invented by Kathryn Gallagher Morton in Newmarket, Ontario. She found success in the late '80s selling *Anne of Green Gables* products before switching in 2003 to producing an exquisitely Canadian alternative to American Girl dolls. The line includes seven dolls, each with her own backstory, hobbies, accessories, and Canadian hometown. Morton's company spent over two years researching Nunavut culture before introducing Saila, who's from Iqaluit. Her parka and hat are made by Inuit craftspeople. Brianne, from Manitoba, loves to dance at the Dauphin Ukrainian Festival and has a pony named Chinook. Léonie, who looks forward to visiting the sap house every March, is an Atom-level hockey player from Quebec City, and no doubt a Youppi! fan.

Ukpik is the Inuktitut word for snowy owl and the inspiration for Ookpiks, small souvenir handicraft owls made of sealskin or wolf fur. They were invented by Jeannie Snowball of northern Quebec in the early '60s. An unlikely Ookpik fad erupted after the cute creations represented Canada at an American trade show in 1964. The wise but goofy creature is a fitting mascot for this country. The federal Department of Northern Affairs and Natural Resources (now Indigenous and Northern Affairs Canada) realized its mascot potential in '64 and presented it to the Northern Alberta Institute of Technology, where most of the sports teams are still called the Ooks.

BONHOMME: SUPER A-LISTER SNOWMAN

At the opening of the annual *Carnaval de Québec*, the mayor hands the key to the city over to the celebration's mascot, Bonhomme Carnaval. A jolly, seven-foot snowman is now the keeper of Quebec City. Not only is he large and in charge, he is the carnival's undisputed celebrity. Unlike the 1988 carnival queen, Isabelle Boutin, who fled from her ball in tears when she perceived she was being outshone by Brooke Shields, Bonhomme cannot be upstaged. Not even a national treasure like Anne

Murray, who danced with him at the 1984 ball, can hold a candle to him. According to studies, he's recognizable to a whopping 96 percent of the inhabitants of *La Belle Province*.

A gregarious, moon-faced fellow with a red cap and sash belt, Bonhomme's official web page lists his stats, much like you would see on a hockey card. Here, we find out that this beloved character was born in Quebec City, he weighs four hundred pounds, his favourite colours are red and white, and his distinctive movement is the leg raise. Yes, this mascot's claim to fame is his ability to stand on one foot. So proud is he of this manoeuvre that it warrants a mention alongside his catchphrase ("Happy Carnival!") and his favourite treat (ice cream and sorbet). The most fantastical line of his bio imparts that Bonhomme "is surrounded

by an air of mystery and most of all, an authentic respect."

Carnaval attendees are encouraged to buy a Bonhomme Effigy, which acts as a passport to all the event's festivities. In English Canada, the word *effigy* is almost always used in the context of the phrase "burned in effigy." That's because the word's most common usage is to denote "a roughly made model of a particular person, made in order to be damaged or destroyed as a protest or expression of anger." At this point, most anglophones would theorize that there is something lost in the French/English translation of the term. Nope. The French word for effigy is *effigie*, and it is commonly employed in the context of burning by using the phrases *exécution en effigie* or *brûlé en effigie*.

This pervasive fire reference must cause tremendous trauma

Bonhomme, the perfect snow gentleman.

for a man of snow, yet partaking in the carnival is Bonhomme's raison d'être. He leads the parades, he waves jubilantly from *calèche* rides, he cheers the icy canoe race across the St. Lawrence, he hugs children and grown-ups alike.

In years past, Hudson's Bay sponsored the carnival's *bain de neige* event, at which swimsuited revellers roll around in the snow. Bonhomme is highly animated while carousing with the bikini-clad participants, but only appropriately so. After all, this is a snowman worthy of "authentic respect," and he conducts himself as such, despite dubious offers: In 1995, *Carnaval* organizers were forced to firmly tell producers of a porn movie called *Quebec Sexy Girls* that they could by no means use the snowman's image in the film.

A Bonhomme controversy erupted again in 2001 when Quebec author Pierre Brisset des Nos released *Les Années Fantômes*, a novel that depicted the cherished symbol of Quebec winter revelry as a gun-toting criminal who smuggled cocaine in his oversized snow head. The book cover depicted the mascot aiming a handgun at a pair of fishnetted legs. *Carnaval* organizers demanded the book be taken off the market and took their case to Quebec's Superior Court. The book publisher countered by accusing *Carnaval* of censorship, telling the CBC, "We're not saying Bonhomme is wicked. This is a novel." In the end, the contents remained unedited, but Bonhomme was removed from the cover.

It is important that his image be protected because Bonhomme's credence has transcended the carnival to the point where he is now a mascot for all of French Canada. Children across the country learn about Bonhomme in elementary French class. He provides a friendly entrance point to learning the foreign ways of our much-loved French compatriots with their gendered nouns, run-on *liaison* words, and their lame churchy swear words. Bonhomme is a beacon of fun among verb conjugations. His enduring popularity means his image is often employed as visual shorthand for the Province of Quebec.

But this is not always a positive thing. *Maclean's* magazine was the focus of country-wide outrage in 2010 when it employed Bonhomme as a totem to illustrate a cover story on

Boomers in denial
They're actually fatter
than their parents P.70

HARPER'S RE-ELECTION PLAN P.12
THE FIGHT OVER FROSH WEEK P.74

Jennifer Lopez
Is she mean enough
for American Idol? P.80

MACLEAN'S

CANADA'S NATIONAL MAGAZINE

OCTOBER 4, 2010

THE MOST CORRUPT PROVINCE IN CANADA

Accusations of influence peddling
in Jean Charest's cabinet are just the
latest mess. Why so many political
scandals happen in Quebec. P.16

An unwilling cover boy.

255

Quebec political corruption. The cover image featured a cheery Bonhomme carrying a briefcase so stuffed with bills that money was flying out its sides. Organizers of *Carnaval* protested against the magazine and claimed they had been duped into agreeing to let *Maclean's* use Bonhomme's likeness under false pretences; they also claimed that the magazine had violated intellectual property rights. "Bonhomme is really, really well known across Quebec and across Canada," *Carnaval* president Jean-François Côté told *CTV News*. "But having been used this way … has a tremendous negative impact on us."

This powerful figure had humble beginnings as the brainchild of Quebec City restaurateur and *Carnaval* planner Louis-Philippe Plamondon. He was always intended to represent and inspire a simple *joie de vivre*, which is the rare and highly sought-after realization that you're enjoying yourself. But is Bonhomme enjoying himself at our expense?

There is a benign breed of internet troll that propagates pranks online for no reason other than fun. For example, the practice of Rickrolling, whereby a friend sends you a link to the latest zoo animal escape caper or gallery of dogs in hot dog costumes, but when you click on the link, you're instead confronted with the video for Rick Astley's 1987 pop hit "Never Gonna Give You Up." It's silly. It's surprising. It's harmless. And there are reasons to believe that Bonhomme is involved in these types of shenanigans.

No, the *Carnaval* snowman is not going to send you a bum link to an '80s video. Bonhomme is much more dry and clever than that. And since *Carnaval* runs only seventeen days of the year, he has the remaining 348 days to mess with us.

Bonhomme's official web page is part of the larger *Carnaval de Québec* site. Naturally, *Carnaval* is active on the five most common and popular social media networks: YouTube, Facebook, Twitter, Pinterest, and Instagram. Bonhomme does not engage in these. Instead, at the bottom of his profile, there is a link that invites you to follow him on LinkedIn, the business-oriented social network. It would be delightfully goofy if the link brought you to the video "Never Gonna Give You Up." But Bonhomme is operating on a whole different level. The link takes you to the snowman's legit LinkedIn profile. First Name: *Bonhomme*. Last Name: *Carnaval*. Current Employer: *Carnaval de Québec*.

Education: *École de la Chute des Neiges*. Interests: *fun*. The result is not *ha-ha* funny, but as you read through Bonhomme's projects, special skills, and the earnest recommendations from his colleagues, you realize this is purely a surprising and generally delightful find, but one that also poses the question *Why?* If this is trolling, then troll on, delightful Quebecois snowman. Your playful whimsy defines *joie de vivre* and represents the best of what's unreal.

Vive Bonhomme! Vive Québec! Et vive ce quiz!

. . . .

1. **When did Bonhomme become *Carnaval*'s mascot?**
   a) 1894
   b) 1927
   c) 1955
   d) 1980

2. True or false: Bonhomme speaks.

3. The word *carnival* comes from the Latin words for
   a) "popcorn" and "to dance"
   b) "meat" and "to put away"
   c) "sleeves" and "to sing"
   d) "snowman" and "to speak"

4. The term *ceinture fléchée* describes Bonhomme's
   a) hat
   b) buttons
   c) belt
   d) boots

ANSWERS

. . . .

1. When did Bonhomme become *Carnaval*'s mascot?

Answer: c) 1955

The *Carnaval de Québec* began in 1894, but went on hiatus during the world wars and through the Depression. The event began to find its footing again in 1945, and by 1955 it had achieved the cohesion it continues to enjoy. *Carnaval* has taken place every year since 1955, the year that the Bonhomme mascot made his debut.

A *Carnaval* brochure from the 1800s.

2. **True or false: Bonhomme speaks.**

Answer: true

According to his web page, "He is a character that moves and dances, expressing his feelings through unique movements." He also expresses himself in both official languages and chats away to visitors and the press alike. During an interview on CBC's *The Hour,* he spoke about the benefits of his regular yoga practice. "It just helps me deal," he maintains.

The mute mascot tradition is attributed to Disneyland, where speaking is against the rules for costumed characters. Disneyland opened on July 17, 1955, five months after Bonhomme first received the key to Quebec City.

3. **The word *carnival* comes from the Latin words for:**

Answer: b) "meat" and "to put away"

Did you know carnivals are Catholic? Yes, these internationally hosted carnal celebrations of meat and mayhem, dancing and drinking, parades and parties, masks and make-out sessions, are part of the wintertime festive season leading into the Catholic season of Lent. Carnivals let those rowdy Catholics get all the partying out of their system before Lent, a forty-day period when (good) Catholics abstain from meat, alcohol, parties, and other treats in the lead-up to Easter. Because of the tradition of giving up meat, the word *carnival* is built out of the Latin words *carne* (flesh or meat) and *levare* (to take away). If you guessed d), "snowman" and "to speak," try a little harder. We're almost at the end, but buck up and try to finish strong, okay? Everybody knows the Latin for talking snowman is *sermo aequaliter nubila hominis.*

• • • • • • • • • • • • • •

4. The term *ceinture fléchée* describes Bonhomme's

Answer: c) belt

Ceinture is the French word for a belt, or a sash tied at the waist. *Flèche* means arrow, and *fléchée* refers to the chevron pattern on this particular type of belt. The *ceinture fléchée* makes a regular appearance in traditional French-Canadian attire going all the way back to the fur-trade days. Tied around a coat's waist, these handmade sashes helped to prevent cold drafts. They are traditionally finger-woven, just like your grade six friendship bracelets, but these suckers are much larger. They're fifteen to twenty-five centimetres wide and easily two metres long, so get weavin'.

THANK YOU

Acknowledgements

Heartfelt thanks go out to my cheerleaders and proofreaders: Mike and Bonnie Villamere, Chris Bailey, Sarah Villamere, Bridget Downing Scime, Kathleen Villamere, Nancy Kelly, Dana Brown, Pauline Villamere, Tayler Villamere, Ruth Villamere, Julie Villamere, Laura Calder, Aidan Compeau, Alice Villamere, Wendy Lavallee, Carroll Calder, Catherine Gray, and Jake Guindon. My woes and I could not have made it through summer '16 without you.

Heaps of appreciation also go to my agent, Carolyn Swayze, and to Kris Rothstein of the Carolyn Swayze Literary Agency, who encouraged me to propose this book, helped me to refine the proposal, and then magically connected me to a book deal.

And what a book deal it was! With Dundurn Press, I experienced a group of professionals who took this goofy book extraordinarily seriously and offered me a level of support and service that just totally blew my socks off. A big thanks goes out to the whole Dundurn team and especially to Allison Hirst, Kathryn Lane, Jenny McWha,

Shout out to Neil Landry, an Ottawa-based photographer and musician who so kindly let me use his terrific Peter Puck shots pro bono for Chapter 18. This is one of my all-time faves.

Jaclyn Hodsdon, Laura Boyle, Carrie Gleason, Margaret Bryant, Sheila Douglas, and Kirk Howard.

Big ups to Adria Lund and the gang at the Glenbow Museum Archives; Mark Furukawa, a.k.a. Dr. Disc, at the best record shop in the Hammer; book trailer creator extrodinare Spencer Barclay;

and to boss Hamilton-based illustrator Ashley Ince.

Most of all, thank you to my husband, Peter Calder, for his unending support and for helping me realize the weird dream of Canada: anything is possible. I hope that carries true for our beloved daughter and inspiration, Bonnie Edith-Anne Villamere Calder.

And last, thanks to those who have come before us to put this country together the best they could. Pierre Trudeau said "A country, after all, is not something you build as the pharaohs built the pyramids, and then leave standing there to defy eternity. A country is something that is built every day out of certain basic shared values." Let's try every day to be totally unreal in the best possible way to build a country that is wise, silly, and ours.

AHHH
LICKY
BOOM
BOOM
DOWN

Appendix

Here, for your reference and reverence, are the full and unedited lyrics of the Canadian classic "Informer," as made popular by Snow.

Informer
You know say Daddy Snow me, I'm gonna blame
A licky boom-boom down
'Tective man says Daddy Snow stabbed someone down the lane

A licky boom-boom down
Informer
You know say Daddy Snow
    me, I'm gonna blame
A licky boom-boom down
'Tective man says Daddy
    Snow stabbed someone
    down the lane
A licky boom-boom down
Police-a them-a they come
    and-a they blow down me
    door
One him come crawl through
    through my window
So they put me in the back
    of the car at the station
From that point on I reach
    my destination
Now the destination reached
    was the East Detention
Where they whipped down
    my pants and looked up
    my bottom
Informer
You know say Daddy Snow
    me, I'm gonna blame

A licky boom-boom down
'Tective man says Daddy
    Snow stabbed someone
    down the lane
A licky boom-boom down
Informer
You know say Daddy Snow
    me, I'm gonna blame
A licky boom-boom down
'Tective man says Daddy
    Snow stabbed someone
    down the lane
A licky boom-boom down
The bigger they are they
    think they have more
    power
They're on the phone me
    say that on hour
Me for want to use it once to
    call my lover
Lover who I'm gonna call is
    the one Tammy
I love her from my heart
    down to my belly
Yes Daddy Snow, I'm the
    coolest daddy

The one MC Shan and the
one that is Snow
Together we are like a
tornado
Informer
You know say Daddy Snow
me, I'm gonna blame
A licky boom-boom down
'Tective man says Daddy
Snow stabbed someone
down the lane
A licky boom-boom down
Informer
You know say Daddy Snow
me, I'm gonna blame
A licky boom-boom down
'Tective man says Daddy
Snow stabbed someone
down the lane
A licky boom-boom down
Listen for me ya better listen
for me now
Listen for me ya better listen
for me now
When I rock the microphone,
I rock it steady

Yes sir Daddy Snow me are
the Article Don
When I'm at a dance they
say, "Where you come
from?"
People then say I come from
Jamaica
But I'm born and raised in
the ghetto
That's all I want you to know
Pure black people man
that's all I man know
My shoes used to tear up
and my toes used to
show
Where I'm born is the one
Toronto, so
Informer
You know say Daddy Snow
me, I'm gonna blame
A licky boom-boom down
'Tective man says Daddy
Snow stabbed someone
down the lane
A licky boom-boom down
Informer

You know say Daddy Snow
    me, I'm gonna blame
A licky boom-boom down
'Tective man says Daddy
    Snow stabbed someone
    down the lane
A licky boom-boom down
Come with a nice young lady
Intelligent, yes she's gentle
    and irie
Everywhere I go I've never
    left here at all
Yes, me Snow roam the
    dance
Roam the dance in every
    nation
You'd never know, me
    Daddy Snow
I am the Boom Shakata
I'll never lay down flat in one
    cardboard box
Yes, me Daddy Snow I'm
    gonna reach to the top, so
Informer
You know say Daddy Snow
    me, I'm gonna blame

A licky boom-boom down
'Tective man says Daddy
    Snow stabbed someone
    down the lane
A licky boom-boom down
Informer
You know say Daddy Snow
    me, I'm gonna blame
A licky boom-boom down
'Tective man says Daddy
    Snow stabbed someone
    down the lane
A licky boom-boom down
Why would he? [repeat]
Me sitting round cool with
    my dibby dibby girl
Police knock my door, lick
    up my pal
Rough me up and I can't do
    a thing
Pick up my line when my
    telephone ring
Take me to the station,
    black up my hands
Trail me down 'cause
    I'm hanging with the

Snowman

What am I gonna do, I'm
black and I'm trapped
Smack me in my face, took
all of my gap
They have no clues and they
wanna get warmer
But Shan won't turn informer
Informer
You know say Daddy Snow
me, I'm gonna blame
A licky boom-boom down

'Tective man says Daddy
Snow stabbed someone
down the lane
A licky boom-boom down
Informer
You know say Daddy Snow
me, I'm gonna blame
A licky boom-boom down
'Tective man says Daddy
Snow stabbed someone
down the lane
A licky boom-boom down

Sources

1: *The Littlest Hobo*: Our German Shepherd Guardian Angel TV Star

CTV. *The Littlest Hobo*. Toronto, 1979–1985.

Hawthorn, Tom. "Chuck Eisenmann, 91, Baseball Player, Dog Educator." *Globe and Mail*, December 28, 2010.

Keith, Ronald. "Canada's Smartest Dogs." *Globe and Mail*, July 29, 1972.

"The Littlest Hobo." IMDb. Accessed June 5, 2016. www.imdb.com/title/tt0078644.

Zyvatkauskas, Betty. "The Word *Mutt* Is Taboo on Toro's Set." *Globe and Mail*, September 22, 1979.

2: Sol: The Hobo Clown of *Parlez-Moi*/Your Nightmares

"Cirque du Soleil Launches Highly Anticipated Sol the Clown Show." *O-Dot, The*, June 21, 2011. http://the-o-dot.blogspot.ca/2011_06_01_archive.html.

Cobb, Christopher. "Sol Plays Now to Overgrown 'Children.'" *Ottawa Journal*, March 18, 1978.

Conogue, Ray. "Bedraggled Clown Deflates Pretensions of High and Mighty." *Globe and Mail*, September 29, 1992.

———. "Just for Laughs' Bread and Butter: *Juste Pour Rire*." *Globe and Mail*, July 22, 1999.

Gavin, Mike. "Red Skelton's Paintings Exhibited at Las Vegas." *Park City Daily News*, June 21, 1964.

Johnson, William. "Sol the Clown's Verbal Amusement Park." *Globe and Mail*, March 8, 1982.

Peterson, Maureen. "A Sunny Performance from Sol and his Puns." *Ottawa Journal*, March 28, 1978.

Scott, Gail. "Quebec's Clown with the Poet's Soul." *Globe and Mail*, June 23, 1973.

Stone, M.J. "Marc Favreau, Entertainer 1929–2005." *Globe and Mail*, February 6, 2006.

3: Wilf Carter: Maritime Cowboy and Hobo Balladeer

"The Case for the Hobo." *Globe and Mail*, February 14, 1938.

Green, Richard. "Country Music." *Canadian Encyclopedia. Last edited June 4, 2014.* www.thecanadianencyclopedia.ca/en/article/country-music-emc.

"The Cultured Hobo." *Globe and Mail*, July 15, 1931.

Evans, Steve, and Rod Middlebrook. *Cowboy*

Guitars. Anaheim: Centerstream, 2002.

"Famous Moments: Hobos." Library and Archives Canada. Accessed June 5, 2016. www.collectionscanada.gc.ca/trains/kids/021007-1070-e.html.

Hodgman, John. *The Areas of My Expertise*. New York City: Riverhead Books, 2006.

Liberman, Anatoly. "On Hobos, Hautboys, and Other Beaus." OUPblog, Oxford University Press, November 12, 2008. http://blog.oup.com/2008/11/hobo.

"Six-Year-Old Hobo: Girl Completes 'Hop' From Lambton Mills to Edmonton." *Globe and Mail*, December 31, 1935.

Tommy Hunter website. "Tommy Hunter." Accessed June 6, 2016. www.tommyhunter.com.

Wadey, Paul. "Obituary: Wilf Carter." *Independent*, December 16, 1996.

West, Bruce. "Vanishing Hobo." *Globe and Mail*, April 22, 1964.

"Wilf Carter." Canadian Songwriters Hall of Fame. Accessed June 5, 2016. www.cshf.ca/songwriter/wilf-carter.

4: *Hobo with a Shotgun*: Vigilante Hobo Canuxploitation A-Go-Go

Barker, Andrew. "Review: *Hobo with a Shotgun*." *Variety*, January 22, 2011.

Canadian Academy of Recording Arts and Sciences. "The JUNO Awards." Accessed June 21, 2016, http://junoawards.ca.

"Paul Gross Plans to Leave Whizbang Films, Which He Co-founded." *CTV News*, August 20, 2012. www.

ctvnews.ca/entertainment/paul-gross-plans-to-leave-whizbang-films-which-he-co-founded-1.922149.

Doyle, John. "Hey Nova Scotia, Way to Kill a Cultural Achievement!" *Globe and Mail*, April 21, 2015.

"Hobo with a Shotgun." IMDb. Accessed June 21, 2016, www.imdb.com/title/tt1640459.

Hobo with a Shotgun website. Accessed June 21, 2016, http://ca.hobowithashotgun.com.

"The Toronto Haunts Michael Cera Loves." *Toronto Star*, August 4, 2010.

Travers, Peter. "*Hobo with a Shotgun." Rolling Stone*, May 5, 2011.

5: The "Beaver Hour": CanCon Quota Gets a Ghetto Slot

"About." JUNO Awards. Accessed August 6, 2016. http://junoawards.ca/about.

Roper, Bob. "The Strange Case of Bryan Adams." *Prime Time*, CBC Radio, September 26, 1991. Hosted by Geoff Pevere.

"Sylvia Tyson on CanCon's Early Years." *Sunny Days*, CBC Radio, August 15, 1975. Hosted by David Parry.

York, Ritchie. "Can a Law Put Canada on the Hit Parade?" *Globe and Mail*, August 24, 1968.

6: Hinterland Who's Who: Cool Flute Tune but Beaver Questions Remain

Boswell, Randy. "Hibernating or Extinct? Original Black-and-White *Hinterland Who's Who* TV spots missing on 50th anniversary." *National Post*, July 9, 2013.

Fabiani, Louise. "The Greatest Environmentalist You've Never Heard Of." *Toronto Star*, April 25, 2013.

"*Hinterland Who's Who* Beaver Vignette Found in Archives." *CBC News*, July 29, 2013. www.cbc.ca/news/canada/british-columbia/hinterland-who-s-who-beaver-vignette-found-in-archives-1.1411232.

Balpataky, Katherine. "*Call of the Wild*." Canadian Wildlife, Winter 2004. Excerpt. www.hww.ca/en/about-us/50th/history.html.

Ohayon, Albert. "Propaganda Cinema at the NFB — The World in Action." NFB/blog, September 30, 2009. http://blog.nfb.ca/blog/2009/09/30/propaganda-cinema-the-world-in-action.

"Pamphlets Have Information on Wildlife." *Chilliwack Progress*, May 3, 1972.

7: *Cucumber*: Moose + Beaver + Tree House = Zero Cukes

"Alex Laurier." IMDb. Accessed July 7, 2016. www.imdb.com/name/nm0491420.

"Andrea Martin." IMDb. Accessed July 7, 2016. www.imdb.com/name/nm0551908.

Boyd, Liona. *In My Own Key: My Life in Love and Music*. Toronto: Stoddart, 1999.

"Catherine O'Hara." IMDb. Accessed July 7, 2016. www.imdb.com/name/nm0001573.

"Dave Thomas." IMDb. Accessed July 7, 2016. www.imdb.com/name/nm0858686.

"Dawn Harrison." IMDb. Accessed July 7, 2016. www.imdb.com/name/nm0365554.

Doucette, Travis. "An Interview with Clive Vanderburgh ("Cucumber" and TVOntario Years, 1974–79)." YouTube video. Posted by "Travis Doucette," June 3, 2013. www.youtube.com/ watch?v=LAiAwYr8g04.

"Heather Conkie," IMDb. Accessed July 7, 2016. www.imdb.com/name/ nm0174673.

"John Candy." IMDb. Accessed July 7, 2016. www.imdb. com/name/nm0001006.

"The More You Know," *Wikipedia*. Accessed July 7, 2016, https://en.wikipedia. org/wiki/The_More_You_ Know.

"Nikki Tilroe." IMDb. Accessed July 7, 2016. www.imdb. com/name/nm0863475.

"Report Canada." IMDb. Accessed July 7, 2016. www. imdb.com/title/tt0275149.

Rick's TV. "Report Canada." Accessed July 7, 2016. http:// rickstv.com/tvo/reportcanada. html.

Smith, Kathleen. "Lights, Camera, Stardom." *Globe and Mail*, August 27, 1985.

8: *The Beaver*: Tittering Pervs Force Mag's Name Change

Adams, James. "The Beaver's Name Passes into History." *Globe and Mail*, January 12, 2010.

Aston, Suzy, and Sue Ferguson. "*Maclean's*: The First 100 Years." Accessed June 28, 2016. www.macleans.ca/about-us/ macleans-the-first-100-years/.

Austen, Ian. "Web Filters Cause Name Change for a Magazine." *New York Times*, January 24, 2010.

"The Beaver Gets a New Name." *CBC News*, January 12, 2010. www.cbc.ca/news/canada/ manitoba/the-beaver-gets-a- new-name-1.865851.

Carcasole, Mark. "Parents Claim York Region School Internet Filters Ineffective;

Pornography Accessible." *Global News*, January 22, 2016. http://globalnews. ca/news/2472413/parents-claim-york-region-school-internet-filters-ineffective-pornography-accessible/.

Green, Jonathon. *The Vulgar Tongue: Green's History of Slang*. London: Oxford University Press, 2014.

Husser, Amy. "'Oh, Canada!' Stephen Colbert Crudely Redefines Our National History." *Vancouver Sun*, February 6, 2010.

Johansmeyer, Tom. "Canada Can't Handle the *The Beaver*." *Gadling*, January 14, 2010. http://gadling. com/2010/01/14/canada-can-t-handle-the-the-beaver/.

Morrison, Deborah. "Happy 90th Birthday *Beaver Magazine*." *Canada's History*, January 2, 2010.

Nickel, Rod. "Canada History Magazine Drops Double-Entendre Name." Reuters, January 12, 2010. http://ca.reuters.com/article/ domesticNews/idCATRE-60B3ZH20100112.

Patriquin, Martin. "How 'The Beaver' Lost Its Name." *Maclean's*, February 17, 2010.

9: *Electric Circus*: Let's Spandex-Dance on TV

MacRae, Dan. "9 Moments of Maximum Electric Circus." *Aux*, July 23, 2015. www.aux. tv/2015/07/9-moments-of-maximum-electric-circus.

Cleary, Val. "Everything's Coming Up Moses." *Maclean's*, August 1973.

Conroy, Ed. "That Time When CityTV Knew Music." blogTO, September 14, 2012. www.blogto.com/

city/2012/09/that_time_
when_citytv_knew_music.

"Electric Circus: Toronto, 1088–
2003." Let There Be House,
December 24, 2011. www.
lettherebehouse.ca/?p=2048.

Johnston, Aidan. "Electric Circus:
An Oral History of Canada's
Greatest Dance Music Show."
Vice, March 4, 2015. www.
vice.com/en_ca/read/ielectric-
circusi-an-oral-history-of-
canadas-greatest-dance-music-
show-675.

Segarini, Bob. "Happy
Anniversary MuchMusic."
Segarini, August 31,
2012. https://bobsegarini.
wordpress.com/2012/08/31/
segarini-happy-anniversary-
muchmusic.

Vermond, Kira. "Former TV
Host Dini Petty Is Starting
a Business Again … at 71."
Globe and Mail, March 9,
2016.

10: Maestro Fresh-Wes: The Backbone of Canadian Hip Hop

Adams, Gregory. "Maestro
Fresh Wes Gets Classified,
the Trews, Rich Kidd for
'Black Tuxedo' EP, Reveals
New Album Plans." Exclaim,
September 17, 2012.

Adams, Trevor J. "Persistence of
Vision." Halifax Magazine,
September 14, 2013.

Andrews, Erline. "New Canadian
Station Seeks Caribbean TV/
film Content." Trinidad and
Tobago Guardian, February 1,
2015.

Cowie, Del. "Maestro Fresh
Wes." Rev. by Andrew
McIntosh. Canadian
Encyclopedia. Last edited
February 14, 2017. www.
thecanadianencyclopedia.ca/
en/article/maestro-fresh-wes.

"Wes Williams." IMDb. Accessed
July 12, 2016. www.imdb.
com/name/nm0661641.

11: Snow: All the "Informer" Info That's Fit To Print

Adrienne Clarkson Presents. CBC. Accessed August 6, 2016. www.youtube.com/watch?v=swjMG3XkrBA.

Ford, Tracey. "Informer." Rolling Stone, June 14, 2012. www.rollingstone.com/music/news/informer-snow.

MacNeil, Jason. "A Tribe Called Red's Ian Campeau Helps Convince Nepean Redskins to Change Name." *Huffington Post Canada, September 19, 2013.* www.huffingtonpost.ca/2013/09/19/a-tribe-called-red-nepean-redskins-change-name_n_3956010.html.

"Reflections on Canadian Reggae Artist Snow 18 Years After 'Informer' Topped the Charts." *Marco on the Bass Blog, January 7, 2011.* http://marcoonthebass.blogspot.ca/2011/01/reflections-on-canadian-reggae-artist.html.

Rice, Waubgeshig. "Electric Powwow." *The Walrus,* November 11, 2013. http://thewalrus.ca/electric-powwow/.

"Snow." *Encyclopedia.com.* Accessed August 6, 2016, www.encyclopedia.com/doc/1G2-3494100078.html.

Snow (Darrin O'Brien). "Expect Snow on Drew Carey." *Suburb Notorious Outrageous Website, September 21, 2002.* www.dsnow.co.uk/site/expect-snow-on-drew-carey.

12: "Wheelchair Jimmy": Started from Degrassi, Now He's Drizzy

Bowman, John. "Heritage Minutes Rap Drake Lyrics in 'Most Canadian Mashup of All Time." *CBC News, March 10, 2015.* www.cbc.ca/news/trending/heritage-minutes-rap-drake-lyrics-in-most-canadian-mashup-of-all-time-1.2989080.

"Drake Opens Members-Only Sher Club at Toronto's Air Canada Centre." *Hello!*, May 11, 2015. http://ca.hellomagazine.com/music/02015050515919/drake-opens-members-only-sher-club-at-toronto-s-air-canada-centre/.

Kohn, David. "The King of Rap." *CBS News, November 18, 2002.* www.cbsnews.com/news/the-king-of-rap.

13: Sir John A. Macdonald: Founder of the "Go home, Dad, You're Drunk" Meme

"Abandonment Issues: Rockwood Insane Asylum." *Jermalism, July 11, 2011.* http://jermalism.blogspot.ca/2011/07/abandonment-issues-rockwood-insane.html.

Bellamy, Matthew J. "Under the Influence." *The Walrus, June 13, 2013.* http://thewalrus.ca/under-the-influence.

Fuhrmann, Mike. "Sir John A. Passed Out Drunk During Fenian Raids." *Toronto Star*, June 19, 2015. www.thestar.com/news/canada/2015/06/19/sir-john-a-passed-out-drunk-during-fenian-raids.html.

Hopper, Tristin. "Everyone Knows John A. Macdonald Was a Bit of a Drunk, but It's Largely Forgotten How Hard He Hit the Bottle." *National Post, January 9, 2015.* http://news.nationalpost.com/news/canada/everyone-knows-john-a-macdonald-was-a-bit-of-a-drunk-but-its-largely-forgotten-how-hard-he-hit-the-bottle.

"Sir John A. Macdonald." Library and Archives Canada.

Accessed August 6, 2016. www.collectionscanada. gc.ca/sir-john-a-macdonald/ index-e.html.

Taylor, Peter Shawn. "A Toast to Canada's First and Funniest Prime Minister." *C2C Journal, June 1, 2015*. www. c2cjournal.ca/2015/06/a-toast-to-canadas-first-and-funniest-prime-minister.

Winsor, Hugh. "A Long Tradition of High Tolerance for Peccadilloes." *Globe and Mail, March 21, 2009*. www. theglobeandmail.com/news/ national/a-long-tradition-of-high-tolerance-for-peccadilloes/article764907.

14: William Lyon Mackenzie King: Inspired Spiritualist, Big, Big Fan of Dogs

"A Séance at Laurier House." CBC Digital Archives. From *Sunday Morning, March 6, 1977*. www.cbc.ca/player/ play/2193782104.

"First Among Equals." Library and Archives Canada. Accessed August 6, 2016. www.collectionscanada.gc.ca/ primeministers/h4-150.18-e. html#a.

King, Mark. "Orlando Is the Cat's Whiskers of Stock Picking." *Guardian, January 13, 2013*. www.theguardian. com/money/2013/jan/13/ investments-stock-picking.

"Mackenzie King's Diaries Released." CBC Digital Archives. Accessed August 6, 2016, www.cbc.ca/archives/ entry/mackenzie-kings-diaries-released.

Martin, Lawrence. "The Weirdo PM Who Showed the Way." *Globe and Mail, November 8, 2011*. www. theglobeandmail.com/ news/politics/the-weirdo-

pm-who-showed-the-way/
article4182988/.

15: Stephen Harper: Hockey Fan, *Murdoch Mysteries* Star

"Born Christmas Day." *Courier-Post, December 31, 1971.*

Carlson, Kathryn Blaze. "Meet Stefania Capovilla, The Hairstylist Behind These Parliament Hill Dos." *National Post, May 9, 2012.* http://news.nationalpost.com/news/canada/meet-stefania-capovilla-the-hairstylist-behind-these-parliament-hill-dos.

Downie, Jim. "Justin Just Like Dad." *Ottawa Citizen, December 24, 1971.* http://j.mp/2aETFth.

Ferreras, Jesse. "Justin Trudeau on Justin Bieber: Stop Teasing Him, He Says in State Dinner Toast." *Huffington Post Canada, March 10, 2016.* http://j.mp/2aSijBO.

Friedman, Vanessa. "Justin Trudeau Takes an Image, and Wins with It." *New York Times, October 1, 2015.* http://j.mp/2aDBu0Y.

Hoffman, Jan. "Justin Bieber Is Living the Dream." *New York Times, December 31, 2009.* http://j.mp/2b1eGNY.

Johnson, Brian D. "Justin Bieber: I Want to Be the Next Michael Jackson." Maclean's, November 21, 2012. www.macleans.ca/culture/the-prince-of-pop.

Paul Fraser Collectibles. "Justin Bieber Authentic Hair Cuttings." Accessed August 7, 2016. http://store.paulfrasercollectibles.com/Justin-Bieber-Authentic-Hair-Cuttings-p/jb-hc.htm.

Pelley, Lauren. "Meet the Woman Behind Justin Trudeau's Hair." *Toronto Star, November 10, 2015.*

www.thestar.com/news/
canada/2015/11/10/meet-
the-woman-behind-justin-
trudeaus-hair.html.

"Rumors Confirmed: Mrs.
Trudeau Expecting, Due
December." *Montreal Gazette,
July 24, 1971.* http://j.
mp/2aMrALb.

Schmunk, Rhianna. "Justin
Trudeau's Hair Returns to
Spotlight in New Liberal
Ad." Huffington Post
Canada, October 17, 2015.
www.huffingtonpost.
ca/2015/10/17/justin-trudeau-
hair-ad_n_8322968.html.

16: Justin Trudeau: #hair

Alphonso, Caroline, and Gloria
Galloway. "The Prime
Minister, the Psychic Stylist
and the Big Flap." *Globe and
Mail*, April 21, 2007. www.
theglobeandmail.com/news/
national/the-prime-minister-
the-psychic-stylist-and-the-
big-flap/article1354371.

Atwood, Margaret. "Stephen
Harper's Hair Problem." *The
Walrus, August 21, 2015.*
https://thewalrus.ca/stephen-
harpers-hair-problem.

"Confederate Treasure." *Murdoch
Mysteries'* Wiki. Accessed
August 6, 2016, http://
murdochmysteries.wikia.com/
wiki/Confederate_Treasure.

Coyle, Jim. "For Stephen Harper,
a Stable Upbringing and
an Unpredictable Path to
Power." *Toronto Star*, October
4, 2015. www.thestar.com/
news/insight/2015/10/04/
for-stephen-harper-a-
stable-upbringing-and-an-
unpredictable-path-to-power.
html.

"Don Cherry to get 'Shawinigan
Handshake' on Beer Label."
CBC News, April 13, 2012.
www.cbc.ca/news/canada/

montreal/don-cherry-to-get-shawinigan-handshake-on-beer-label-1.1280999.

Hopper, Tristin. "The Nerd Who Came from Nowhere." *National Post*, August 13, 2015. http://news.nationalpost.com/news/canada/canadian-politics/the-nerd-who-came-from-nowhere-stephen-harper-knows-you-dont-need-to-like-a-politician-to-elect-him.

Ort, David. "Shawinigan Handshake a Hoppy Wheat Beer from Quebec." *Post City Toronto, July 11. 2013*. www.postcity.com/Eat-Shop-Do/Eat/July-2013/First-Draught-Shawinigan-Handshake-a-hoppy-wheat-beer-from-Quebec.

Selley, Chris. "Stephen Harper's Long-Awaited Hockey History Is Exhaustive, Exhausting." *National Post, November 5, 2013*. http://news.nationalpost.com/full-comment/chris-selley-stephen-harpers-long-awaited-hockey-history-is-exhaustive-exhausting.

Simpson, Jeffrey, and Brian Laghi. "Incremental Man." *Globe and Mail, October 4, 2008*. www.theglobeandmail.com/news/politics/incremental-man/article1063376.

17: Hidy and Howdy: Twin Rodeo Polar Bears

Allen, Scott. "The Weird and Scary History of Winter Olympic Mascots." *Mental Floss*, February 14, 2010. http://mentalfloss.com/article/23958/weird-scary-history-winter-olympic-mascots.

Gandia, Renato. "Hidy and Howdy Honoured with

Entry into Canada's Sports Hall of Fame." *Calgary Sun*, March 1, 2013. www.calgarysun.com/2013/03/01/hidy-and-howdy-honoured-with-entry-into-canadas-sports-hall-of-fame.

"International Polar Bear Day Celebrations!," *Fuzfeed*. Accessed August 6, 2016, https://fuzfeed.com/international-polar-bear-day.

Haynes, Dave. "Bears Sigh with Relief." *Calgary Herald*. Accessed August 8, 2016, http://calgaryherald.com/uncategorized/day-15-hidy-and-howdy-via-calgary88live.

Krause, Darren. "Hidy and Howdy." *Metro News, February 14, 2013*. www.metronews.ca/features/calgary/1988-calgarys-olympic-moment/2013/02/14/hidy-and-howdy-i-think-

they-became-the-face-of-the-games.html.

Powell, Mike. "The Strange Evolution of Olympic Mascots." *Windsor Star*, May 19, 2010. www.windsorstar.com/travel/ideas/snow-sports/Photo+Gallery+strange+evolution+Olympic+mascots/3052455/story.html.

Steinberg, Neil. "The New Science of Cute." *Guardian*, July 19, 2016. www.theguardian.com/world/2016/jul/19/kumamon-the-new-science-of-cute.

"Winter Olympics Mascot Is Named." *Journal-News*, September 12, 1979.

18: Peter Puck: The *Itchy & Scratchy* of Hockey
Hockey Hall of Fame. "Peter Puck." Accessed August 6, 2016. www.hhof.com/htmlTimeCapsule/t7humour.shtml.

"Jason Cavalier." IMDb. Accessed August 6, 2016. www.imdb.com/name/nm0146767.

"Jacques Plante." *Historica Canada*. Accessed August 8, 2016. www.historicacanada.ca/content/heritage-minutes/jacques-plante.

Posner, Michael. "A Reluctant Author of Bestsellers." *Globe and Mail, March 17, 2009.* www.theglobeandmail.com/arts/a-reluctant-author-of-bestsellers/article973347.

"Time of Your Life." IMDb. Accessed August 1, 2016. www.imdb.com/title/tt0396385.

19: Youppi! The Ultimate Free Agent

Campbell, Murray. "Turning the Page." *Globe and Mail.*

Gupta, Anika. "The Woman Behind Ms. Piggy." *Smithsonian Magazine*, October 2008. www.smithsonianmag.com/arts-culture/the-woman-behind-miss-piggy-11290861.

Jermyn, Diane. "Canadian Doll Maker Faces Tough Competition Against American Girl." Globe and Mail, August 21, 2015. www.theglobeandmail.com/report-on-business/small-business/sb-growth/the-challenge/american-girl-dolls-out-to-usurp-canadian-counterparts/article26002154.

Kesterton, Michael. "World o' Mascots." *Globe and Mail.*

Wyatt, Nelson. "Youppi, Rare Orange Lobster, Dies." *Huffington Post Canada*, November 18, 2011. www.huffingtonpost.ca/2011/11/18/youppi-the-miracle-lobste_n_1102052.html.

"Youppi." NHL.com. Accessed August 3, 2016. http://

canadiens.nhl.com/club/page.
htm?id=59287.

**20: Bonhomme: Super A-Lister
Snowman**
Bonhomme Carnaval.
"Bonhomme Carnaval."
LinkedIn. Accessed August 1,
2016. www.linkedin.com/in/
bonhommecarnaval.
CBC Digital Archives. "Brooke
Shields Outshines Carnival
Queen." Accessed August 6,
2016. www.cbc.ca/archives/
entry/brooke-shields-
outshines-carnival-queen.
"Cover of *Maclean's* Magazine
Causes Controversy." *CTV
News*, September 24, 2010
http://montreal.ctvnews.ca/
cover-of-maclean-s-magazine-
causes-controversy-1.556410.
"The Life of Bonhomme."
YouTube video. From
The Hour. Posted by
"Strombo," February 16,
2009. www.youtube.com/
watch?v=M3ormLOk7Dk.
"Quebec Carnival Hires Lawyers
to Protect Bonhomme." *CBC
News, September 27, 2010.*
www.cbc.ca/news/canada/
montreal/quebec-carnival-
hires-lawyers-to-protect-
bonhomme-1.922696.
"Rogers Regrets *Maclean's*
Bonhomme Cover." *CBC
News*, September 30, 2010.
www.cbc.ca/news/canada/
montreal/rogers-regrets-
maclean-s-bonhomme-
cover-1.963643.

Image Credits

157 Frederick M. Brown/ Getty Images, http://j. mp/2b46KfA. All rights reserved. Used with permission.

158 Kevin Winter/Getty Images,
(left) Editorial #: 452250510. All rights reserved. Used with permission.

158 Jag Gundu/Getty Images,
(right) http://j.mp/2aExALg. All rights reserved. Used with permission.

159 Elsa/Staff, Getty Images Sport, Editorial #: 510108134. All rights reserved. Used with permission.

160 Neilson Barnard/Getty Images for MTV, Editorial #: 177928030. All rights reserved. Used with permission.

166 Library and Archives Canada 3000462, item e008072622. Used with permission.

168 Library and Archives Canada 3624840, item PA-025746. Used with permission.

170 Library of Congress Prints
(left) and Photographs Division. Brady-Handy Photograph Collection. Call number: LC-BH83-555.

170 Library and Archives
(right) Canada 4168383, item 3010930930. Used with permission.

174 Underwood and Underwood, New York, http://j.mp/2aDLCH4.

182 Library and Archives Canada 3217522, item C-009059. Used with permission.

183 Library and Archives
(left) Canada 3192217, item C-024304. Used with permission.

183 Library and Archives
(right) Canada, 3940022, item e010782428. Used with permission.

188   Library and Archives Canada, 3192217, item C-024304, https://flic.kr/p/aD1APZ. Creative Commons Attribution 2.0 Generic.

192   AFP/Getty Images Editorial #: 51395210. All rights reserved. Used with permission.

194   *Calgary Herald* — Mikael Kjellstrom, CW7758904.

196 (top)   Claus Andersen/Getty Images Editorial #: 461088776. All rights reserved. Used with permission.

196 (bottom)   Helm/Getty Images, Editorial #: 470757720, All rights reserved. Used with permission.

205   Library and Archives Canada 3192217, item e011084047. All rights reserved. Used with permission.

207   Asclepias, http://j.mp/2aWhsQJ, Creative Commons Attribution-Share Alike 3.0 Unported.

211   Jesse Grant/Getty Images for iHeartRadio/Turner. All rights reserved. Used with permission.

216–17   Ashley Ince. All rights reserved. Used with permission.

218   Mike Powell/Allsport, Getty Images Sport, Editorial #: 1220343. All rights reserved. Used with permission.

219 (left)   Glenbow Museum Archives, Image No: NA-5654-32. All rights reserved. Used with permission.

219 (right)   National Archives of Canada C-027645.

222   http://bit.ly/2jKW2wj, Creative Commons Attribution NoDerivs 2.0 Generic.

Index

Eaton's, 46, 125
EDM (electronic dance music), 122, 123, 125
Einstein, Bob, 22
Eisener, Jason, 58
Eisenmann, Chuck, 24, 25
Electric Circus, 117–27, 130, 134
Electric Circus (nightclub), 125, 126
Elizabeth II, Queen, 173, 175
Erickson, Bonnie, 240, 245, 247, 248
Erickson, E. Albert, 248
exploitation films, 53, 58. *See also* Canuxploitation
Expo 67, 239

Fallon, Jimmy, 246
Famous Chicken, 241, 245, 247
Favreau, Marc, 27–26
Feist, 223, 224
Ferrier, Garry, 70
FEVA TV, 137
Fichman, Niv, 59
50 Cent, 75, 153
Flex, Farley, 135, 137
FLOW 93.5 FM, 137
"Flute Poem," 79, 81, 86, 87
Ford, Rob, 133
Four Lads, The, 68
Foxx, Jamie, 163

Fraggle Rock, 96
Freeman, Stan, 125

Gallant, Patty, 76
Game, The, 153
gangsta rap, 152–54, 157, 160
Ghostbusters, 187–89
Giannoulas, Ted, 247
Gibson, Debbie, 118, *119*
Giuliani, Rudy, 173–74
Glyn-Jones, David, 23
Goldberg, Joel, 120, 130
Gosling, Ryan, 161, 163
Gowan, Lawrence, 135, 136
Graham, Aubrey Drake. *See* Drake
Grantis, Donna, 97, 101
Grealis, Walt, 75
Greene, Lorne, 68, 87, 187, 189, 233, 237
Gretzky, Wayne, 157, 195, 211
Grey, Deborah, 197, 199
Grey Cup, 191, 236
Grindhouse, 24, 58, 59
Gross, Paul, 60
Guess Who, The, 70, 76, 133

Hammerman, 154
Hanna-Barbera, 230, 231
Harper, Stephen, 133, 191–201, 204, 208, 213